KENT BL

N.

ORNAMENT

Published by
Yale School of Architecture
180 York Street, New Haven, CT 06520
www.architecture.yale.edu

Distributed by
Yale University Press
302 Temple Street
PO Box 209040
New Haven, CT 06520-9040
www.yalebooks.com/art

This book was made possible by the Yale School of Architecture. It is based on the symposium, "The Natures of Ornament," held in February 2019.

We would like to acknowledge all the participants in the symposium and the work of A.J. Artemel and Richard DeFlumeri who made it all happen.

Editors: Sunil Bald and Gary Huafan He
Publications Director: Nina Rappaport
Copy editor: Ann Holcomb
Graphic Design: Office of Luke Bulman
Printed by Regal Printing in China

ISBN: 978-0-300-25471-6

Library of Congress Control Number: 2020934999

The Kent Bloomer Scholarship was established by: Stephen W. Harby (BA '76, MArch '80), Tina Beebe (MFA '74), and Robert "Buzz" J. Yudell (BA '69, MArch '73)

With additional support from: Kevin Dale Adkisson (BA '12), Jacob D. Albert (BA '77, MArch '80), Marc F. Appleton (MArch '72), Paul B. Bailey (MArch '72), Bruce R. Becker (MArch '84, MBA '85), Charles Bergen (BA '85, MArch '90), Kent C. Bloomer (MFA '61) and Leonor G. Bloomer (MA '77), Mary F. Burr (MArch '14), Josephine Bush, John B. Clancy (MArch '96), Raymond and Marilyn Gindroz, George Craig Knight (MArch '95), Mariko Masuoka (BA '78, MArch '80), Ann K. McCallum (MArch '80), Julia H. Miner (MArch '80), James V. Righter (MArch '70), Brent Sherwood (BA '80, MArch '83), Georgia M. Todd (MArch '17)

KENT BLOOMER
NATURE AS
ORNAMENT

Edited by Sunil Bald and Gary Huafan He

Yale School of Architecture

New Haven

Distributed by Yale University Press
New Haven and London

III. STUDIO

IV. LEGACIES

V. PLACES

FOREWORD

Sunil Bald

Sunil Bald is associate dean at Yale University School of Architecture. He is a partner in the New York-based Studio SUMO, which was awarded the Annual Prize in Architecture from the American Academy of Arts and Letters in 2015.

Natures of Ornament is published in honor of Kent Bloomer who taught at Yale School of Architecture for over fifty years and influenced thousands of students, both undergraduates and graduates. His influence is undeniable and lives through both his work as a practitioner and his interactions with others as a scholar, colleague and teacher. This impact is reflected in both the enthusiasm and range of contributions contained in this volume. The four sections—Histories, Cosmos, Legacies, and Place—are meant to reflect ornament's expanse in time and space, and also the reach of Kent's work as a thinker, writer, and maker.

While Bloomer has been a fixture within the School of Architecture, his role has always been to challenge architecture's disciplinary nature through his suspicion of dogma. He consequently proudly positioned himself as an *ornamentalist,* a term that describes his work, but brings discomfort to those aligned with architecture and pedagogy grounded in canonical Modernism. I admit at first feeling that discomfort myself, when we began our decade-long teaching partnership—an arranged marriage, formed by Dean Robert A.M. Stern. Kent and I were joined together to teach the newly conceived and required visualization course to incoming MArch I students. Our union quickly became conspiratorial as I was introduced to the conceptual richness of Kent's approach. Situated within the ego of a design studio and the superego of Peter Eisenman's formal analysis course, we embraced the role as the Id of the first semester curriculum. We meshed Kent's decades of expertise teaching geometric principles that are increasingly glossed over in curricula by the power and agility of technical tools that provide everything without requiring an understanding of basic ideas that can be used to create complexity. We fine-tuned a sequence of exercises, usually crafted over a single shared large coffee divided into two cups, and a single shared brownie sliced diagonally, that Kent delightedly characterized as *diabolical.* It has been through Kent that I have come to understand the academic value of the diabolical. I have also come to understand something about Kent. Kent began to teach at Yale in 1967, the year that *The Graduate* was released. In one resonant scene, a building supervisor played by Norman Fell asks Dustin Hoffman, the recent graduate who was trying to rent a room in Berkeley, "You're not one of those agitators, are you?" I am quite sure that Charles Moore brought Kent Bloomer to Yale that year *because* he was an agitator—not one who upends the system, but someone who needles it from the inside.

And it is here that *The Nature of Ornament* and the "Nature of Bloomer" uncannily merge. Ornament itself plays the role of agitator, bound to structure but visually vibrating in space. Foliation, appropriation, metamorphosis, and above all rhythm, these are restless words that put our built world in motion and agitate its sense of stolidity. Relative to the locus of Modernism and the primacy of structure, form, and function, ornament has been marginalized within the modern academy. Consequently, ornament has had to operate as an opportunistic infiltrator that has recently re-emerged with a force. Kent etymologically ties ornament to the Greek word *Kosmeo,* which means to arrange, to order, to adorn, emerging in today's parlance in the word "cosmetics." But Kent embraces and extends this line of inquiry to the word *Kosmos,* and positions ornament as "a force that transforms conflicting worldly elements."

It is in this spirit that Gary He and I, with Kent's continued input, curated the contributors to this volume, bringing together a diverse collection of voices to interrogate ornament's many forms, roles, manifestations—both worldly and otherworldly—and, in its many natures, the spirit of joyful agitation that ornament and Kent Bloomer have contributed to these intersecting scholarly spheres.

I. HISTORIES

TASSELS, TAPESTRIES, AND TEMPLES: ORNAMENT AS THE ORIGIN OF ARCHITECTURE

Mari Hvattum

Mari Hvattum is professor of architectural history and theory at The Oslo School of Architecture and Design, where she teaches modern architectural history and theory.

I have always found that the so-called "Vitruvian tradition"—a tradition marked more by its eighteenth- and early nineteenth-century protagonists than by Vitruvius himself—operated with a rather uninspired idea of ornament. The French academician Antoine Chrysostome Quatremère de Quincy, for instance, described ornament as a "secondary embellishment," used to "add a clearer significance to . . . the character of an edifice"—in other words, not doing much.[1] The Swedish-British architect William Chambers was even more unimaginative: in his 1759 *Treatise on Civil Architecture*, he presented ornament as something of an afterthought in the history of architecture. The first buildings had no trace of ornament, Chambers argued; they were "rough and uncouth."[2] Only after generations and generations did any kind of ornament enter the picture in the form of moldings. Ornament, it seems, is an add-on: a nice but potentially disposable embellishment onto a body that is perfectly capable of standing unadorned.

It is, to be sure, a perfectly sensible argument: first you build something and make sure it stands up, then you decorate it. Structure is primary; adornment is secondary. There are, however, dissenters to this commonsensical hierarchy—rebellious voices who have insisted on turning the relationship between structure and ornament resolutely on its head. This little piece is dedicated to them.

Adornment as the Origin of Architecture

My first rebel is the German architect and architectural historian Karl Bötticher. Not an obvious choice, perhaps: Bötticher's famous *Die Tektonik der Hellenen* (1844–52) seems very much to align itself with the Vitruvian tradition, presenting ornament precisely as a secondary embellishment, subservient to and expressive of the architectural structure.[3] But Bötticher has another side to him, revealed in one of his lesser known books, *Der Baumkultus der Hellenen* (1856). Writing on Greek tree cult, Bötticher went back to a time before architecture, tracing the beginnings of the temple, not in the primitive hut or some other rustic building, but rather in the ephemeral arrangements in and around sacred trees. These were "the first temples to the gods," he proposed, preceding architecture proper.[4]

What made the trees in the Greek tree cult sacred, Bötticher argued, was their ritual adornment. He wrote about wreaths and ribbons as the oldest forms of such adornment, describing how these motifs originated in the ritual, ossified gradually into the ornament, and finally entered into the architectural ensemble in a gradual process of transfiguration. Architecture, here, is not a matter of building first and adorning after, and it is certainly not about the conventional hierarchy of structure and ornament, so often associated with Bötticher. What comes to the fore is a far more quirky, original, and imaginative way of thinking about the role of ornament in architecture—understanding it more as an ossified gesture than a secondary embellishment. And more: the ornament is the origin of architecture, preceding the building, both chronologically and ontologically.

Ornament as Ossified Gesture

If, for neo-classicists like Chambers and Quatremère de Quincy, the building preceded its adornment, for Bötticher in *Der Baumkultus der Hellenen* (1856), it was precisely the opposite (figure 1). A man who shared this conviction and developed a whole theory of architecture on the basis of it was the German architect and theorist Gottfried Semper. The motifs of adornment, Semper argued, were far older than architectural construction and existed long before architecture proper. Take the wall, for instance. For Semper, the wall had essentially nothing to do with load bearing, but was "the architectural element that represents and makes visible enclosed space as such."[5] This is not an abstract space, however, nor is it a space of pure extension, as Semper's modernist readers have sometimes rendered it.[6] Rather, it is a space defined by ritual practice and articulated by ornament. The original enclosure was the wickerwork wall, Semper argued, a motif that soon metamorphosed into the woven screen whose patterns revealed the method of its fabrication. Semper wrote about the way the varying color of the grass stalks created variation in the weave, and how that variation was gradually utilized to create patterns.[7] He discussed the repetitive movement of the loom as an imitation of natural rhythms, interpreting the ornamental patterns in the weave as part of architecture's mimetic function. It is this mimetic capacity that makes weaving—together with other rhythmical phenomena such as the dance, the scroll, the beating of oars—a means to visualize and partake in a cosmic order.[8] The ornament is the origin of architecture: the first materialized attempt at representing the physical world in human-made form.

In this way of thinking, it is not the ornament, but rather the load-bearing structure that is an afterthought. Semper considered the structuring of the spatial enclosure incidental, "foreign to the original architectural idea," as he put it.[9] Monumental architecture, he insisted, springs from the ephemeral ornamentation, not the sturdy tectonics of the load-bearing structure:

> The festival apparatus . . . enhances, decorates and adorns the glorification of the feast, and is hung with tapestries, dressed with festoons and garlands, and decorated with fluttering bands and trophies—these are the motives for the permanent monument.[10]

Throughout history, the textile enclosure with its ornamental patterns metamorphosed into other materials: Assyrian stone reliefs, Chinese latticework, Roman mosaics. Yet in all its iterations, the enclosure retained its ornamental vocabulary, continuously echoing its textile origin.

Semper paid an almost obsessive attention to the ornamental physiognomy of the textile wall and its metamorphoses (figure 2). He discussed the seam and the knot—analyzing their formal, technical, historical, and symbolic properties, and demonstrating their ornamental expression in textiles and architecture alike. He analyzed the hem, both as a finishing fold in a fabric and as an ornamental structuring device in the architectural facade.[11] He delved into crochet and embroidery, spinning and felting, exploring the way the symbolic and structural aspects of these techniques metamorphosed into the architectural ornament. Personally, I have always found one of the most endearing passages in *Der Stil* (1860–3) to be the section on tassels, i.e., the ornamental edge of a fabric or indeed a wall. Semper went through different edge conditions in his usual obsessive detail, comparing, for instance, the Doric triglyph with the jagged edge of a fabric "cut with shears to prevent the unraveling . . . of unhemmed textile edges," that is, both as a technical necessity and a visual completion of the ornamental field.[12] He is nothing if not radical, discussing even the most sturdy stone wall—such as the ashlar wall of Palazzo Pitti—as an ornamental fabric:

> These stone dressings were stylistically dependent on the art of wall finishing (textiles) . . . because the symbolism of any cover, following the most ancient tradition, derived from or conformed with decorative forms that came from processes such as weaving, plaiting, embroidery, and edging.[13]

Ornament Rebellion

There is a delicious dismantling of neo-classical origin theory going on here. Rather than locating the essence of architecture in the structural solidity of stone or wood, Semper located it in the most delicate needlework. It is a way of thinking that turns the hierarchy of structure and ornament on its head—proposing the wonderfully counterintuitive thesis that the most ephemeral decoration precedes the most sturdy wall, and that architecture's monumental structures originate in flowing fabrics.

I like to imagine Kent Bloomer as someone who has continued the rebellious tradition from Semper and Bötticher—rebelling against the reduction of ornament to an afterthought and insisting, instead, that ornament harbors the very idea of architecture.

Notes

1. Antoine Chrysostome Quatremère de Quincy, "Ornement" in *Dictionnaire historique d'architecture* (Paris: Librairie d'Adrien le Clere et Cie, 1832), vol. 2, 179–81.

2. Sir William Chambers, *A Treatise on Civil Architecture, in Which the Principles of That Art Are Laid Down and Illustrated by a Great Number of Plates, Accurately Designed, and Elegantly Engraved by the Best Hands* (London: J. Haberkorn, 1759), 2.

3. Karl Gottlieb Wilhelm Bötticher, *Die Tektonik der Hellenen* (Potsdam: Riegel, 1852).

4. Bötticher, *Der Baumkultus der Hellenen nach den gottesdienstlichen Gebräuchen und den überlieferten Bildwerken dargestellt* (Berlin: Weidmannsche Buchhandlung, 1856), 9.

5. Gottfried Semper, *Style in the Technical and Tectonic Arts; or, Practical Aesthetics*, trans. Harry Francis Mallgrave and Michael Robinson (Los Angeles: Getty Research Institute, 2004), 247. Original edition: *Der Stil in den technischen und tektonischen Künsten, oder Praktische Ästhetik*, vol. 1: Frankfurt am Main: Verlag für Kunst und Wissenschaft, 1860; vol. 2: Munich: Friedrich Bruckmann's Verlag, 1863.

6. See, e.g., discussions of De Stijl's reading of Semper in Michael White, *De Stijl and Dutch Modernism* (Manchester: Manchester University Press, 2003).

7. Semper, *Style*, 248.

8. Ibid., 82.

9. Ibid., 248.

10. Ibid., 249.

11. Ibid., 729–30, 737.

12. Ibid., 125.

13. Ibid., 736–37.

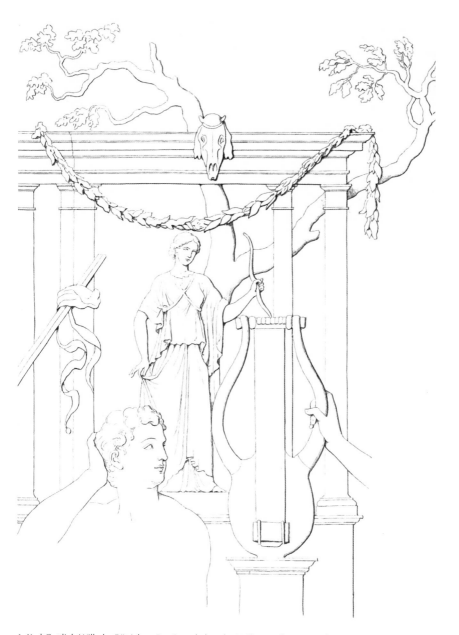

1. Karl Gottlieb Wilhelm Bötticher, *Der Baumkultus der Hellenen*, plate 58. Berlin: 1856.

und ihre gleiche Bedeutung bei allen, als Kunstsymbol, sowie in mystisch-religiöser Beziehung. — Ich habe einige Beispiele derartiger Symbole, den verschiedensten Zeitaltern und den einander fremdesten Nationen angehörig, soweit sie mir gerade zur Verfügung standen, zusammengestellt zu kürzester Erläuterung meiner Vermuthung, dass die Gemeinschaftlichkeit eines natürlichen und daher überall nothwendig gleichen Ausgangspunktes der Technik zu der Erklärung der merkwürdigen formellen Uebereinstimmung dieser Symbole bei allen Völkern nicht ausreicht.

Aegyptisches Pflanzengeschlinge.

§. 19.

Die Naht als Kunstsymbol.

Die Naht ist von dem oben besprochenen Bande struktiv und

2. Gottfried Semper, *Egyptian Vegetal Ornament in Der Stil in den technischen und tektonischen Künsten*, vol. 1, p. 84. Frankfurt am Main: Verlag für Kunst Wiseenschaft, 1860; Munich: F. Burckmann, 1863.

GLOBAL CHIPPENDALE: THE CIRCULATION OF ORNAMENT IN THE EIGHTEENTH CENTURY

Stacey Sloboda

Stacey Sloboda is associate professor of art at the College of Liberal Arts at University of Massachusetts, Boston. Her areas of expertise are eighteenth and nineteenth century visual and material culture, history and theory of design and decorative arts; cross-cultural artistic contact; histories of collecting and display.

In a brief but suggestive article published in 1966, the historian Mark Girouard noted the existence of "two worlds"—those of fine art and craft practices—in St. Martin's Lane in the eighteenth century.[1] Indeed, the neighborhood converging upon and surrounding this tiny, serpentine street in the heart of London (figure 1) was the center of artistic training and community for two generations of British painters, sculptors, and architects including William Hogarth, Francis Hayman, Richard Wilson, Samuel Scott, Allan Ramsey, Joshua Reynolds, Johann Zoffany, the sculptor Louis-François Roubiliac, and the architects James Paine and William Chambers. Most of these men were directly involved as instructors, members, or students of the St. Martin's Lane Academy, which had been reopened by Hogarth and the portrait painter John Ellys in 1735. In addition to these fine artists, the illustrator Hubert-François Gravelot, gold chaser George Michael Moser, and the medalist Richard Yeo were principal instructors at the Academy. At the same time, by mid-century, the best-known cabinetmakers and wood carvers of the period, including Thomas Chippendale, John Channon, William Vile and John Cobb, William Hallett, William and John Linnell, Matthias Lock, Thomas Johnson, and Benjamin Goodison all had workshops in or directly around the lane.

This roll call of names confirms Girouard's identification of this neighborhood as what we might call today an arts district, cultural quarter, or what Vic Gatrell identifies as "the world's first creative 'bohemia'," while Girouard notes that, "the whole business of the connection between artists and craftsmen at this period deserves further research."[2] Intrigued by this claim, I began looking for those connections and thinking about their significance. To do so, I've mined a range of archival sources, particularly the pattern books, drawings, and other designs that were made in this neighborhood. It is my contention that the ornament we find in those designs is a key source for uncovering a rich series of social and creative networks that formed a remarkable and stylistically coherent artistic community. Through the ornament which it produced, we see in this mid-eighteenth-century London neighborhood not "two worlds" of fine art and craft practice, as Girouard's intriguing claim had it, but one world of overlapping, collaborative, and competitive networks of artists, artisans, suppliers, dealers, patrons, and institutions which made up the London art world of the time.

One example that begins to reveal the meaningful artistic connections facilitated by various design practices in St. Martin's Lane can be found in the career of Matthias Lock, a master carver based in Long Acre, just around the corner from St. Martin's Lane. Little is known of Lock until he published *Six Sconces*, a pamphlet of six design drawings in 1744, which was the first extant Rococo pattern book made and published in England. Lock followed the success of this publication with a second book, the ingeniously named *Six Tables*, in 1746, which demonstrates the carver's increasingly fluid, inventive, and sophisticated two-dimensional designs (figure 2). This period happens to be the precise moment at which George Michael Moser, a drawing master and gold chaser, became the principal instructor at the St. Martin's Lane Academy. Moser overlapped, and then assumed teaching responsibilities from Hubert-François Gravelot, the immigrant French draftsman who also served as a drawing master at the St. Martin's Lane Academy from the early 1740s until he returned to France in 1745. Gravelot was the single figure most associated with the introduction of the French *genre pittoresque*, or Rococo, style to England. Both Gravelot and Moser's work emphasized fluid, animated lines with a particular focus on figural ornament. It seems more likely than not that Lock, a carver newly successful as a published designer and eager to capitalize on the increased social status of being a named artist, availed himself of Gravelot and Moser's life drawing sessions just around the corner, and the increasingly elaborate nature of his published designs are the result of this experience.

The Academy was thus the impetus for fostering a design culture in mid-eighteenth-century London, but it was through printshops that it was disseminated. At least eleven printsellers, among them those most frequently linked to the sale of Old Master and ornamental prints from the Continent, were located in or immediately around St. Martin's Lane in the mid-eighteenth century, including Celeste Regnier who married the sculptor Louis-François Roubiliac in the 1750s, as well as Francis and Susan Vivares.[3] Lacking a strong institutional center to organize or dictate artistic developments, prints were an important vehicle through which artists and artisans—even when they were close neighbors—communicated artistic ideas to one another. My contention is that ornament itself was a vehicle through which artists and artisans forged connections and articulated creative affinity.

In the narrow and rich milieu of St. Martin's Lane, the skills of
a print engraver and those of a wood carver yielded some overlap,
and the simpler medium of etching made printmaking more accessible
to artists with primary skills in both drawing and carving. In some
instances, artists worked and dealt in both furniture carving and
printmaking. Matthias Lock etched and printed many of his own
publications.[4] James Pascall, the carver of a magnificent pair of
girandoles now at Temple Newsam (figure 3), carved furniture and sold
prints from his shop at the Golden Head in Long Acre, immediately
around the corner from St. Martin's Lane. His widow Ann continued
the print business from James's death in 1747 until 1754.[5] The dog
upon Pascall's girandole is the same pooch found in Matthias Lock's
1746 design, who is also seen in the slightly earlier ornamental design
by Hubert-François Gravelot.[6] The direct correspondence between
Lock's design and Pascall's carving—and the fact that they lived just
around the corner from one another—has led some to credit Lock
as the designer of Pascall's furniture.[7] It is a reasonable proposition,
though given Pascall's access to published designs from the Continent
and neighbors alike, it is also possible that he designed his own works,
freely borrowing from printed sources.

These artistic connections, forged through both proximity and print,
can be seen repeatedly in the overlapping design sources, references,
and styles that emerged in St. Martin's Lane in the mid-eighteenth
century. A rare surviving scrapbook of an otherwise unknown London
wood carver named Gideon Saint indicates the tremendous range
of design prints collected by mid-eighteenth-century London artisans,
and the extent to which they used them as inspiration for their own
designs (figure 4).[8] Saint's shop, like Pascall's and many other artists
and artisans in the neighborhood, hung the sign of the Golden Head
in Princes Street near Leicester Square, a few minutes' walk from the
printshops and other wood carvers and cabinetmakers of Newport
Street, Long Acre, and St. Martin's Lane. His book is organized by
furniture type, suggesting that it functioned as both a sketchbook and
design catalogue for potential clients. It includes hundreds of examples
of Continental and English Rococo ornaments cut from prints and
books and pasted in and amongst (presumably) Saint's own pencil
sketches. Those sketches borrow iconography and spirit from other
English and French published designs, sometimes (but not always)

directly copying them. The etched ornaments on this two-page spread are cut from published designs by Thomas Johnson, while the red chalk drawing is a particularly lively copy of another of Johnson's well-known designs.[9] Thomas Johnson was a master carver and designer who published wildly imaginative Rococo designs beginning in the 1750s from his workshop in Queen Street. He was mentored as a draftsman and carver by Matthias Lock in the 1740s when both were working in the workshop of the cabinetmaker James Whittle in Great St. Andrew's Street, to the immediate north of St. Martin's Lane in the Seven Dials.[10] On the opposite page of Saint's book, an exuberant frame comprised of acanthus leaves, C-scrolls, pediments, vases, figures, and the now-familiar hound show Saint bringing together the motifs and styles of Lock and Johnson, as well as Lock's sometime collaborator, H. Copland, who was deeply influenced by, and sometimes copied, the work of Hubert-François Gravelot.[11] And this is just one page of a massive book. Taken as a whole, Saint's book is, in effect, itself a social network that employs ornament as its language.

The intertwined network of artists and artisans in St. Martin's Lane fostered a remarkable number of carvers' and cabinetmakers' ambitions as published designers. By the early 1750s, an obscure cabinetmaker living just at the end of St. Martin's Lane in Northumberland Court named Thomas Chippendale took note of this trend. In collaboration with the engraver and designer Matthias Darly, Chippendale produced an ambitiously large collection of designs, which he published in 1754 from his new address in the heart of St. Martin's Lane as *The Gentleman and Cabinet-Maker's Director*. The subsequent use of Chippendale's name as a metonym for the modern style he espoused is indicative of the extraordinary reach of the book, which was quickly reprinted as a second edition in 1755, and then expanded to a third edition and published in French in 1762 (figure 5). In many ways, Chippendale was just one more artisan participating in the St. Martin's Lane milieu of maker-designers who realized the potential of print as a tool in artistic communication, collaboration, exhibition, and marketing.[12] In other ways his work is unique because of its global scope, as it influenced carvers, cabinetmakers, and patrons across the Continent, in the Americas, and in key Asian locales.

In the 1760s a remarkable number of London-trained artisans made their way to Philadelphia, lured by Pennsylvania's booming economy in agriculture and transatlantic trade. This migration supported the development of a vibrant art world in Philadelphia that both directly referenced, and departed from, London fashion, particularly with the development of the style commonly referred to as Philadelphia Chippendale. London-trained, Philadelphia-based artisans included the carver Hercules Courtenay, who prior to his arrival in town was apprenticed to the St. Martin's Lane carver and designer Thomas Johnson, at the very moment in the late 1750s in which Johnson was publishing the patterns that would later be compiled into *One Hundred and Fifty New Designs*. By 1765, he was indentured to the Philadelphia cabinetmaker Benjamin Randolph.

Randolph's trade card (figure 6), which would have served as an advertisement for his shop, indicates the orientation of his business and his evident need to employ St. Martin's Lane-trained carvers. The trade card is a vibrant collage of Rococo designs and ornaments taken directly from three separate St. Martin's Lane pattern books: Chippendale's *Director* and Johnson's 1758 *Designs for Furniture*, as well as *Household Furniture in the Present Taste . . . by a Society of Upholsterers*, a pattern book published in London in 1760 that compiled previously published designs of Chippendale and Johnson, as well as designs by Robert Manwaring, William Ince and John Mayhew, all of whom worked in the vicinity of St. Martin's Lane. It is likely that Courtenay would have brought those books, or his own scrapbook that included those designs, with him from London to Philadelphia. Randolph may have had access to his employee's books and design collections, or could have acquired them through the local bookseller Robert Bell, or the Library Company of Philadelphia, which owned a copy of Chippendale's 1762 *Director*, and to which Randolph, along with at least eight other Philadelphia cabinetmakers, was a subscribing member.

Cabinetmakers such as Randolph satisfied their elite patrons' desires for technologically advanced furniture in the latest metropolitan styles. At the same time, local and widespread colonial resistance to England's economic dominance, and attendant boycotts on London imports, created a market for Philadelphia artisans to supply sophisticated furniture in London style, by London artisans, but made in Philadelphia. This was not always a straightforward matter of import substitution; instead, Philadelphia Chippendale was also sometimes a colonial hybrid, in which new work emerged from a process of creative adoption and adaption of metropolitan forms and styles. Nowhere is this more apparent than in the form of the American high chest.

In London, the high chest was a baroque form comprising a flat-topped chest of drawers set upon six turned legs. It was largely out of fashion by the first decades of the eighteenth century. In New England, cabinetmakers adapted this form by adding a scroll top with a central drawer, a large central bottom drawer, reducing the number of legs to four, and updating them with a carved cabriole form. The form continued to develop in Philadelphia in the 1750s and 1760s when a carved appliqué cornice replaced the pediment drawer and additional carved panels appeared on the skirt. The splendid example formerly known as the "Pompadour Chest" (figure 7) perfectly exhibits these characteristics, blending a distinctly colonial form with direct references to metropolitan designs. A similar broken pediment with scroll and acanthus leaf volutes, a finial bust, and draped urns appear in No. 107 and 108 of the third edition of Chippendale's *Director*, while the serpent-and-swan motif in the central bottom drawer adapts a design published in Johnson's 1762 *A New Book of Ornaments*. While the chest has not yet been attributed to a specific cabinetmaker or carver, there is no doubt that it is the work of a London-trained Philadelphia carver with ready access to St. Martin's Lane designs.

Those same printed designs traveled beyond the transatlantic world to Asia through the mercantile networks of the East India trade. Furniture workshops in India and China that catered to local merchant and elite demand, as well as the export trade, were well established by the middle of the eighteenth century. At Vizagapatam, on the eastern Coromandel coast of India, Indian cabinetmakers developed a new hybrid style of furniture that married European forms with Indian materials and carving techniques to become known as Anglo-Indian furniture. Workshops in Vizagapatam were established by Indian artisans who were familiar with the skills of ivory working that had been developed earlier in Orissa. Perhaps drawing up on the model of Dutch settlements on the Coromandel coast and in Ceylon, which had an *Ambachtskwartier* or "craftsmen's quarter," the cabinet-making industry in Vizagapatam was clustered on what is now Beach Road, with other workshops operating on the coast in Waltair.

One magnificent example is a series of chairs commissioned by at least two separate English patrons (figure 8). The back splat comprises interlocking S and C curves capped with serpent heads inspired directly from Plate 16 of the 1762 edition of Thomas Chippendale's *Director.* Copies of Chippendale's pattern book and other English designs circulated in India, and Indian craftsman also had access to such designs through furniture supplied by clients as models.[13] Adopting the iconic cabriole leg, claw-and-ball feet, and fluid, curvilinear back splat made the chair immediately recognizable as Chippendale in form, while the novel serpent heads on the splat and rail, as well as the incised decoration in black lac and gilding upon a smooth white ivory veneer, announce it as Indian in style.

The specificity of place, and the possibility of imagining the object and its ornament as both a product and a point of contact between two places, is further revealed in this ivory and rosewood cabinet on a stand made in Vizagapatam around 1765. The form derives from an earlier eighteenth-century English piece, likely supplied by a British patron to a cabinetmaker in Vizagapatam who both widened and elongated the body and claw-and-ball feet. Like the previously discussed chair, ivory inlay articulated with incised black lac replaces decoration that would have been carved in relief from the carcass wood on an English example. The floral border framing the front two doors is similar in treatment to floral chintz patterns made in the region's nearby textile workshops. The eleven drawers of the cabinet (eight are hidden by the doors on the front) are incised with architectural scenes set in generic Arcadian landscapes and the British countryside. The drawers at the top, by contrast, depict a rather surprisingly specific place, Montagu House, then the site of the British Museum, which opened in 1753 in Russell Street, London. The scenes are taken directly from prints made from watercolors by the St. Martin's Lane artist Samuel Wale for the 1761 book, *London and its Environs Describ'd.* The provenance of the cabinet reveals no special familial relationship to Montagu House, making it likely that the image functioned, along with its form, as a reference to England, while its material and decoration referred to India.

These examples of ornament, originated in one place and adapted in others, suggests that, indeed, ornament can exist apart from its application. In fact, it can get up and travel, and be transformed in the process. Kent Bloomer has observed that "the realm of ornament is not just a place of gathering but is also a place in which dismemberment and combination are sanctioned."[14] The Philadelphia and Vizagapatam examples of St. Martin's Lane designs demonstrate this creative, iterative process of dismemberment and combination as a product of social movement in a colonial context. David Pullins has further called this phenomenon "the mobile image." He argues that the logic of cut and paste that emerged from artisanal workshop production was a central feature of a range of artistic practices in mid-eighteenth-century France, and these examples suggest that the practice was even more widespread.[15]

Notes

1. Mark Girouard, "The Two Worlds of St. Martin's Lane," *Country Life* (3 February 1966): 224–27. The article was the third in Girouard's series, "English Art and the Rococo," published in *Country Life* in January and February 1966.

2. Vic Gatrell, *The First Bohemians: Life and Art in London's Golden Age* (London: Penguin Books, 2013), xi; Girouard, "Two Worlds," 225.

3. Other printsellers included Samuel Harding, Samuel Wale, John Pine, Thomas Jefferys, James and Ann Pascall, Charles Grignion, Nathaniel Smith, George Bickham, Jr., and John and Mary Ann Rocque.

4. Lock's original solo publications of the 1740s indicate only his own name and invoke copyright protection. Many of the extant copies of his work were reprinted by Robert Sayer in 1768, after Lock's death in 1765.

5. *Daily Advertiser* (16 June 1740).

6. Desmond Fitz-Gerald, "Gravelot and his Influence on English Furniture," *Apollo* 90 (August 1969): 143–47.

7. Anthony Wells-Cole, catalogue entry for the Temple Newsam girandoles in *Taking Shape: Finding Sculpture in the Decorative Arts*, ed. Martina Droth (Leeds: The Henry Moore Institute, 2008), 97; David Hill, "James Pascall and the Long Gallery Suite at Temple Newsam," *Furniture History*, vol. 17 (1981), 71.

8. Morrison H. Heckscher, "Gideon Saint: An Eighteenth-Century Carver and His Scrapbook," *The Metropolitan Museum of Art Bulletin* 27:6 (February 1969): 299–311.

9. The two etchings on the upper and lower right of page 179 appear in Plate 14 of *One Hundred and Fifty New Designs* (London: Robert Sayer, 1761), a compilation of Johnson's designs of the 1750s, while the two etchings on the left of page 178 appear in Plate 38. The red chalk drawing is printed in this compilation in Plate 52, and was realized as a wall light now in the Philadelphia Museum of Art.

10. On Johnson, see Jacob Simon, *Thomas Johnson's "The Life of the Author"* (London: Furniture History Society, 2003); Helena Hayward, "Newly Discovered Designs by Thomas Johnson," *Furniture History* XI (1975): 40–2; and Hayward, *Thomas Johnson and the English Rococo* (London: Alec Tiranti, 1964).

11. H. Copland's *A New Book of Ornaments* (London: H. Copland, 1746).

12. Anne Puetz usefully identifies the design print as a public exhibition space for mid-century artisans. See Puetz, "Drawing from Fancy: The Intersection of Art and Design in Mid-Eighteenth-Century London," as well as "The Emergence of a Print Genre: The Production and Dissemination of the British Design Print, 1730s–1830s" (PhD thesis, Manchester Metropolitan University, 2007).

13. A copy of Chippendale's *Director* was advertised for sale in the *India Gazette* on January 31, 1785. Amin Jaffer, *Furniture from British India and Ceylon: A Catalogue of the Collections in the V & A and the Peabody Essex Museum* (London: Victoria & Albert Publications, 2001), 197, 200.

14. Kent Bloomer, *The Nature of Ornament: Rhythm and Metamorphosis in Architecture* (New York: W.W. Norton, 2000), 86.

15. David Pullins, "Cut and Paste: The Mobile Image from Watteau to Robert" (PhD diss., Harvard University, 2016).

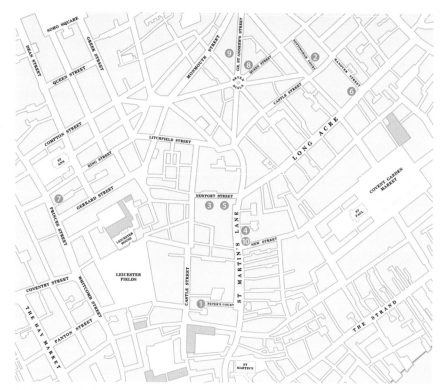

1. Map of Saint Martin's Lane: (1) St. Martin's Lane Academy, Peter's Court; (2) Matthias Lock; (3) Celeste Regnier; (4) Louis- François Roubiliac; (5) François and Susan Vivares; (6) James and Ann Pascall; (7) Gideon Saint; (8) Thomas Johnson; (9) James Whittle; (10) Thomas Chippendale.

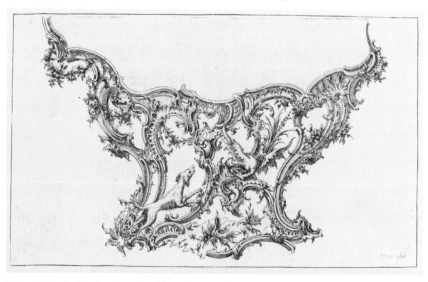

2. Matthias Lock, title plate from *Six Tables*, etching. London: 1746.

3. James Pascall, *Girandole, from the Gallery Suite.* UK: Leeds Museums and Art Galleries, Temple Newsam House, 1745.

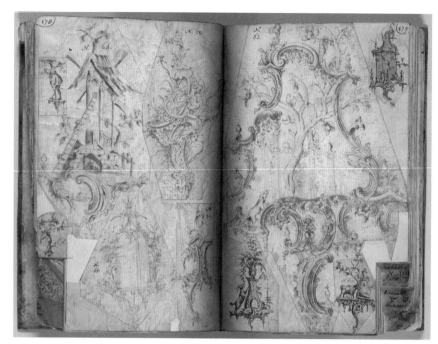

4. Gideon Saint, *Scrapbook of Working Drawings*. UK: 1760.

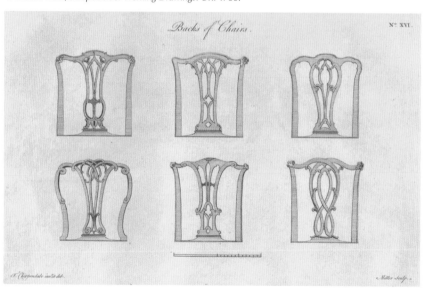

5. Thomas Chippendale, *Backs of Chairs*, from "The Gentleman and Cabinet Maker's Director." London: 1754.

6. James Smither (engraver), *Benjn. Randolph Cabinet Maker, at the Golden Eagle in Chesnut Street Between third and fourth Streets, Philadelphia: Makes all Sorts of Cabinet & Chair work. Likewise Carving, Gildings & c. Performed in the Chinese and Modern Tastes*. Philadelphia: 1769.

7. *High Chest of Drawers*, mahogany, mahogany veneer, tulip poplar, yellow pine, white cedar.
Philadelphia: 1762–65.

8. Artists in Vizagapatam, *India Side Chair*, sandalwood, inlaid ivory, cane, and lac. Vizagapatam, India: c. 1770.

GOING OVER THE EDGE WITH KENT BLOOMER: ORNAMENT RECONFIGURED

Edward Casey

Edward Casey is distinguished professor of philosophy at Stony Brook University, and was the president of the American Philosophical Association (Eastern Division) from 2009–10. He works in aesthetics, philosophy of space and time, ethics, perception, and psychoanalytic theory.

Ornament articulates . . . times and places . . . [It] marshals extremes . . .
to bring many distinct actions into one limited composition.
—Kent Bloomer, *The Nature of Ornament*, 231–32.

Kent Bloomer—architect, sculptor, educator—has created a quiet
revolution with his meditations on the meaning of ornament and by his
concrete praxis of contributing to diverse built places that feature
his original, ornamental designs. He is indisputably the leading theorist
of ornament in our era. In that capacity, he offers much to think about.
In this essay, I examine one strand of his many explorations: that
of *edge* as it intertwines with ornament, forming what Plato calls an
"indefinite dyad," which is composed of the same and the different,
the like and the unlike, the odd and the even.

I

We tend to think of edges as largely utilitarian features of physical
things. In this capacity they are considered to mark the endings of
these things: where they expire as physical substances, the place
of their effective disappearance from perceptibility, where they "fall
off" or "peter out." Edges, thus construed, are regarded as sheer ter-
minations: the end of the story, with nothing more to be said because
there is *nothing more there*. However plausible this view of edges
may seem to be, it represents an arbitrary foreclosure of a more
complete story that needs to be told.

This more complete account includes a discussion of three distinc-
tions that are critical to a fuller understanding of edges: edge vs. limit,
border vs. boundary, active vs. passive edges.

(1) *Limits* are formal determinations that possess a denumerable
quantitative dimension and that are established by standard measures
of one sort or another (scientific calibrations in science, limit states
of gases and solids, etc.). *Edges*, in contrast, may not be subject to any
such exact determination; they can be radically indeterminate (Where
is the edge of the earth? Where do the Rocky Mountains begin?
Where is the edge of my wrath?) and yet still serve as effective edges:
the edge of the earth, even if ambiguous in terms of the precise
parameters of the biosphere, is effectively present in its encirclement
by oceans and continents; the Rocky Mountains emerge in a certain

region of the plains of eastern Colorado even if there is no one spot that amounts to their determinate place-of-origin; my wrath is not endless: it will diminish with time, even if it is difficult to determine the actual moment at which we can say it "no longer exists."

(2) *Borders* are species of limits established either by international agreements (as in the case of the U.S.-Mexico border that was posited in the Treaty of Guadalupe Hidalgo in 1848) or by claims to exact property claims. Not only are they quantitatively specified, they effectively establish the terms of an agreement between two or more parties to the effect that what lies on one side of a given border is a distinctly different domain of land or sea or air than what lies on the other side; borders serve as historically determined interfaces between regions of the earth. *Boundaries*, in contrast, are porous and allow the flowing of people, animals, and plants across them. They possess shape, yet this shape is inherently labile: think of the way a given bioregion allows for the interchange of water, winds, weather, and vegetation with other contiguous regions. Boundaries are edges that are subject to modification, thanks to their own resources and internal forces (whereas borders can only be changed by external fiat: e.g., a new treaty).[1]

(3) *Passive edges* are pre-established, as it were; their fate is settled, at least for the foreseeable future. They do not change themselves from their own internal forces. Borders are examples of passive edges that require intervention from beyond their immediate purview. So, too, are the edges of the table on which I am writing; they are not able to change themselves, even if they are subject to change by external forces and to deterioration over time: in this latter case, they are the passive subjects of such deterioration. *Active edges* are something else again: they refuse to stop at the termination of their surface, their literal vanishing point. Instead, they draw our attention onward—*through* them and often *beyond* them, sending our look (or other form of conscious attention) elsewhere. To this extent, we can say that active edges are self-eclipsing, exceeding themselves, as it were. This happens whenever our bare glance, instead of stopping at the edge of the edge—its apparent, physically presented outer

shape—is sent elsewhere: to what surrounds the edge, its immediate circumambience, that which is contiguous with it, or further afield. The human glance, ever restless and probing, employs edges as stepping-stones to what can no longer be said to belong to a given edge, as such.

With the idea of active edge, we are at the antipode of where we started out. Active edges are not sheer terminal points—visual or tactile cliffs, as it were. Viewed as passive, they do fit this description; but, as active, they are self-exceeding. More basically, they are *animating presences* that redirect the intentionality that first takes them in by a bare noticing. They animate not only our look but the scene in which they are set, not just putting it in a different light but revealing whole swales and swatches of an expanded perception: a literal peri-perception, seeing (feeling, touching, tasting) beyond what is centrally or focally perceived.[2]

II

One way to think about ornament is to say that it is what transfigures limit into edge, border into boundary, and passive into active edges. Although ornament is often found *at the edge* of a given house, temple, or crafted object, it is no mere occupant of that edge. It acts to transform the edge into a dynamic force of its own. Instead of merely marking the end of something—a wall, a door, a dome— it volatilizes what might otherwise be a listless perimeter into some-thing with an inherent force of its own: a force that is not only visual, but haptic (insofar as it invites touch) and kinetic (as inviting move-ment through it). This is conspicuously the case with classical Greek capitals, whose Ionian and Corinthian exfoliations act to complicate what would otherwise be a mere juxtaposition of the edge of a column and that of a roof beam. Mere contiguity turns into the flowing force of configured contours. The same goes for the elaborate edges of certain picture frames. What might be something merely functional or utilitarian here emerges as having a life of its own. So much is this the case that certain painters—notably, Seurat, Marin, Miró, and Hodgkin—have continued their paintings right onto the frame, incorporating the frame into the painting and the painting into the frame. This two-way action is a literal inter-dynamic, a transduction of the frame by the painting and vice versa. In cases such as these, a literally containing edge has been overtaken by a central painted image which, transferred to the frame, *ornaments it*: turns it into something of intrinsic ornamental value.[3]

A comparable instance is that of the ornamental marginalia of medieval manuscripts. As Michael Camille demonstrates in his book *Image on the Edge: The Margins of Medieval Art,* these peripheral images do not merely illustrate or supplement the textual content, they act to subvert it dynamically by their often grotesque imagery of monsters, illicit sexual activity, and more. In other words, they animate a text that, taken literally, is often the essence of piety and orthodoxy, by converting the Word into Image, Logos into Cosmos. This is not just free play made possible by open margins, but a protest at the level of the image—which here forms an alliance with the edge of the page. Camille argues that the authority of the Catholic Church acted both to safeguard the sacred words of the text (e.g., a passage from the Bible or a learned commentary on it) *and* invited its own undermining by allowing its literal marginalia a free hand. Camille sums this up: "Gothic marginal art flourished from the late twelfth to the late fourteenth century by virtue of the absolute hegemony of the system it sought to subvert."[4]

Such examples offer ample evidence of ways by which what might otherwise be a literal edge-as-border is transformed into edge-as-boundary by the interposition of ornament. Thanks to ornament as sculpted form, extended painting, and marginal images, boundary-making proliferates. A capital, a painting frame, the margin of a Gothic manuscript—each exhibits the inherent power of boundaries that emerge in the very face of an otherwise minimal or reductive border-ing. They bring to our attention in compressed formats what can also happen in the case of entire regions—as, for instance, in the case of La Frontera, the name given to the cultural and linguistic landscape that has emerged during the last century and a half at the U.S.-Mexico border. Aptly named "borderlands" by Gloria Anzaldúa—a word that merges both border and boundary in one expression: border/lands—this is the roughly defined area that is spread tenuously but tenaciously on both sides of the *linéa divisoria* that is an international border-line as such. It includes many interlinguistic and intercultural phenomena: it is a hybrid place-world with its own unique identity. As Anzaldúa remarks:

> Borders are set up to define the places that are safe and unsafe, to distinguish *us* from *them*. A border is a dividing line, a narrow strip along a steep edge.

> A borderland is a vague and undetermined place created by the emotional residue of an unnatural [border]. It is in a constant state of transition.[5]

It is all the more striking that this sheer line is sometimes marked by a border wall built right on top of it: as if one kind of edge (sheerly linear qua institutional) calls for another (at once architectural and defensive). This is an edge-to-edge juxtaposition whose primary character is that of demarcating limits—limits of trespassing, of citizenship, of elementary hospitality. The energies of edgework are reduced to deliberately de-limited structures: to an invisible and sheerly projected line or to a highly visible and fiercely fortified wall.

Given the hegemony of state power that is embodied in a border wall, it is therefore not trivial that one side of the wall—significantly, the Mexican side—has become the scene of mural making at various points. Such wall painting is reminiscent of the ways in which the painters I cited earlier took their paintings right onto the frame—only now the place of the frame is taken by a wall (and a wall is, in the end, a frame in its own assertive and defiant way: it frames a nation-state, putting armor-plating around those it is supposed to "protect" and excluding those whose admission it seeks to prevent). Just as tellingly, both at La Frontera and at the Separation Barrier in Israel, there are stretches of the wall—again on the side of those excluded—where there are painted scenes of the landscape one would witness, were no wall to preclude the view. Here the frame is imagined as taken away altogether and replaced by open landscape: a vista that is composed of a series of receding permeable edges. Both kinds of resistant wall art are instances of turning what is intended to be an entirely static edge—a stationary wall—into a dynamic active edge of protest. Anzaldúa puts it this way: "Border artists inhabit the transitional space of *nepantla*. The border is the locus of resistance, of rupture, and of

putting together the fragments."[6] In the case of border art, we witness
in three dimensions a form of active resistance that occurs in two
dimensions in medieval manuscripts. In both cases, it is as if the edge,
rather than merely surrounding an insouciant surface, takes on a life
of its own—a life of defiant resistance to authority, whether this be
religious in the guise of the Catholic Church or secular in the form of
the United States of America.

The edges I have just discussed are not only instances of borders
transformed into boundaries but of edges that have become ornaments—
ornaments in all their subversive potential. But how can an edge be
an ornament?

III

So far, we've been able to observe how edge should not be confused
with limit, nor border with boundary, nor passive with active edges.
Ornament in Bloomer's dynamic and autogenous sense is closely
affiliated with one member of each of these dyads. (a) Far from being
a literal limit—where something sheerly stops—it is de-limiting,
opening up modes of spatial presentation that exceed the literal limits
that are at stake in a *re*presentation that is grounded on the literalities
of resemblance. (b) Instead of establishing or reinforcing a strict border,
ornament creates boundaries that are open-ended and trans-morphic—
converting an eidetic form (a literal pattern) into a creative venture. In
their capacity as boundaries, edges are capable of presenting significant resistance to oppressive regimes of religious or state power. (c) All
such exceeding of limit and border embody the way in which merely
passive patterns—e.g., the "stencil" version of ornament—can take on
active force. From being a merely duplicative or reproductive instance
of *natura naturata,* ornament as active becomes *natura naturans:*
nature becoming actively naturing, nature as *becoming* in the strong
sense given to this word by Bergson and Deleuze.

Ornament as active edge gets ahead of itself, adumbrating the
next twist or new version of a given motif. As Bloomer and Jesperson
put it: "ornament is made up of generative figures that are distributed
into a finite portion of the decorated body. "It is brought forth by
"small figures (nuclei) which we occasionally describe as 'phenomenal
generators'."[7] The language of genesis is significant: when effectively

presented, ornament is not something settled; it is in a continually
nascent state of becoming: becoming other than itself as fixed or static.
In Alfred Whitehead's language, it is a matter of reality — in this case,
built or crafted reality — that is *becoming process.*

Such processive becoming is what active edges accomplish. They
move themselves and that which they ornament into an always-new
next stage, and this is so even if the ornamental design itself moves in
a circle and repeats itself: for the eye or hand does not return to what
is identical but to what is *same qua different.*[8] As Deleuze puts it, it is
a matter of an "active repetition."[9] In their generative energy, ornamental edges repeat themselves, but always with an active difference that
is felt or seen.

IV

The very design that is presented in ornament and attracts and pleases
our eye or hand depends on the delineation of its edges: on their exact
configuration, their pattern, their gestalt or schema. But this is so only
insofar as the recognizable form generates change from within itself
and is thus composed of dynamic edges that alter with time. But let
us be clear: ornament is not just constructed from such edges; it is all
about edges; indeed, *it is all edges* — active and dynamic ones that
don't act just to identify what Whitehead calls "simple locations," but
give rise to open-ended, multiplex places. Ornament is topomorphic,
and it serves to make us topophilic.

Even if much ornament is located at the literal edges of things —
on lintels, the tops of columns, the perimeter of bowls — it can also
appear in the center of that which it ornaments: on whole ceilings,
on entire surfaces of boxes or buildings. This fact does not reduce its
edge-specificity. Not only is every ornament, no matter where it is
located, composed of the discrete edges of its design but, as adorning
any surface, it not only decorates it but activates energetic forces
that transform it. Indeed, it converts *the surface itself into an active
edge* — an edge no longer regarded as the outer periphery of something but as a force in its own right.

Here we reach the antipode of where we began in this essay: edge
as the dead end of physical things. Now the entire surface of the thing
or place effloresces into the effective equivalent of an edge thanks to

the dynamics of its energy and force. This process is itself an instance of the conversion of passive into active edges; but now we take edge itself to a new place; it is no longer the literal outer edge of a given surface, but the transformation of the surface itself into an edge. Taken to the limit—taking all surfaces of a single building together—we reach the point where "the entire building can be an ornament."[10]

Thus, if it is true that ornament "colonizes" "liminal zones" and "boundaries innate to places and structures," such as "the transitional space between things such as column and beam, roof and sky, inside and outside,"[11] this means that ornament prospers in the conjunctures between surfaces of many kinds (built, landscape-bound, earth/sky): it seeks to complicate these conjunctures by its "double 'inside-out' nature"[12]—by overlaying an existing set of given edges with another set of edges that belong to ornament itself: to its very contours and lineaments. This is to edge beyond edge itself. But expansive edges can equally well colonize whole surfaces that exist between given edges, endowing these latter with an enhanced edge-structure that transforms an otherwise barren surface into an entire "decorative field" (in Jesperson's term, taken over from Owen Jones).

Such a field, thus structured, counts as a *place* in the original sense of *chora* as that which receives all things and provides positions for them.[13] It also acts as a (w)edge between other places in the configuration of a region of places, giving them shape (an "outside") by virtue of its acting as their effective "inside." It thereby ornaments them even if it bears no trace of decorative detail as such. For it "claims space by a visually dynamic rhythm rather than by a Cartesian extension."[14] This rhythm is precisely that of the "double 'inside-out'" whereby a given place is both inside other places that are contiguous with it, while being outside each of them taken *seriatim*. If "the purpose of ornament is to momentarily locate ourselves in a much larger place,"[15] this larger place is the choric region composed of several interstitial places. In taking us there, ornament takes us to a world or *cosmos* that is the de-totalized totality of a group of places and surfaces that are its constituent features. It edges into this world by being the kind of active edge that transcends its own finite characteristics and thereby becomes other-to-itself, animating the entire self-transcending series: edges/surfaces/places/regions/world. At once generating and superintending this cosmic series is ornament as Kent Bloomer has taught us to identify, understand, and appreciate it.

V

In short sum: *active edges form boundaried edge-worlds*. Despite the fact that such worlds come in many discrete forms, there are two major *kinds* of them. In one, chaos (*khaos*: abyss) rules supreme. In the other, we encounter cosmos (*kosmos*: order and beauty). Edges figure in the chasm of chaos by way of a sheer proliferation that does not result in any evident coherence, engendering a special anxiety that stems from fearing that no coherent pattern of figures or objects will emerge from the proliferation. At the same time, edges are integral to cosmoi, considered as ordered worlds that display harmonious and non-threatening edges that co-ordinate closely with each other—the effect being beauty of a special sort that derives from the co-inherence of edges with each other. Such edges do not close down or close off, as is the case with limitative or restrictive edges such as we find in borders; they serve to draw together and to open up. Rather than repelling, they attract. We are talking about beauty-in-and-of-the edge.

  A premier instance of edges that contribute centrally to the creation of cosmoi are ornamental edges. These are animated edges that act to trace their own pathways. Not merely embellishing, they offer mini-worlds that are emblematic of an auto-generative ordering that does not depend on utility alone. They are edge phenomena in two basic ways: first, their tracery (in the form of the linearity of autogenous, actively repetitive shape) consists in edges, elegantly and intriguingly arranged; then, the whole ornamental complex constitutes an edge of its own—and as such is set in a special space on a wall or other surface of a building (e.g., at the top): a space that is itself a very special kind of edge, one no longer reducible to the outside perimeter of things. In both capacities, ornament creates spaces of repose, thanks to "pausing" (in keeping with the *pausare* root of "repose": *repausare*) in visual perception rather than rushing to meet goals of efficiency and functionality. In that pause—at once temporal and spatial—an autogenous edge-world can come forward and induce visual and kinesthetic repose.

Ornamental edges do not act merely to close up or terminate—
to stop what is happening at the literal limit of the perceived design.
Instead, in their literally cosmetic powers they lead the eye onward:
not to a different space or time but to a different way of being in the
space-time of the field of their own presentation. They emblematize
what Winnicott labels "transitional space," a figuration that consists in
an exemplary liminality. The *limen* or threshold is itself an edge, but
an edge that leads the eye or hand, and sometimes the whole body,
through to another place that exceeds the very edge of the ornamental
design as such. This is the place of ornament itself, which animates
whatever space or surface it graces.

Ornament so considered contributes centrally to the creation of
a coherent edge-world: a cosmos of beauty and order in which edges
con-figure and co-inhere in patterns that, instead of inducing anxiety,
encourage aesthetic *composure*, a close cousin to the repose induced
by pausing. One pauses at and with ornamental edges and finds
oneself com-posed in psyche and spirit in ways that are uniquely
generated by each ornamental pattern.

* * *

We can conclude that edge and ornament are coeval members of
an indefinite dyad whose interactions are virtually unlimited. They are
same and different, odd and even, like and unlike. In this essay,
I have touched on several of the dyadic relationships they form—
including those adumbrated by Kent Bloomer in his seminal discussions of the meaning and importance of ornament at every stage of
human history, including the present moment, when its survival is
very much at stake. Considered as actively transformative edge-work,
ornament is not the way back, it is the way out and beyond.

Notes

1. For further on the distinction between borders and boundaries, see Edward S. Casey, *The World on Edge* (Bloomington: Indiana University Press, 2017), 7–27.

2. On the peripheral power of glancing, see my study *The World at a Glance* (Bloomington: Indiana University Press, 2007), Part Four: "Praxis of the Glance."

3. For my further discussion of this situation, see "Frames in/of Painting," *The World on Edge*, 97–105.

4. Michael Camille, *Image on the Edge: The Margins of Medieval Art* (London: Reaktion Books, 1992), 160.

5. Gloria Anzaldúa, *Borderlands/LaFrontera: The New Mestiza* (San Francisco: Aunt Lute Books, 2007), 25. Her italics. In my citation, I have substituted "border" for "boundary."

6. Anzaldúa, *Light in the Dark: Rewriting Identity, Spirituality, Reality*, ed. A. Keating (Durham: Duke University Press, 2015), 47.

7. Kent Bloomer and John Kresten Jesperson, "Ornament as Distinct from Decoration," *T3XTURE* no.2 (2015), 23.

8. I here draw upon Heidegger's observation that the Same as a generative force prospers from including Difference—whereas the formally or metaphysically identical strictly excludes Difference. See his late seminar on "Identity and Difference."

9. See Gilles Deleuze, *Repetition and Difference*, trans. Paul R. Patton (New York: Columbia University Press, 1994), Chapter II: "Repetition for Itself," 70–128.

10. Kent Bloomer, *The Nature of Ornament: Rhythm and Metamorphosis in Architecture* (New York: W. W. Norton, 2000), 210.

11. Bloomer and Jesperson, "Ornament as Distinct," 24.

12. Ibid.

13. See Plato's *Timaeus* 50a–52c.

14. Bloomer and Jesperson, "Ornament as Distinct," 34.

15. Ibid., 35

II. COSMOS

ORNAMENT IN BIOTIC AND HUMAN ARTWORLDS

Richard O. Prum

Richard Prum is director of Franke Program in Science and the Humanities and curator of Ornithology and head curator of Vertebrate Zoology in the Yale Peabody Museum of Natural History. He is an evolutionary ornithologist with broad interests in avian biology.

Introduction

The biological sciences have participated in rich interactions with aesthetics and aesthetic philosophy since the early-nineteenth-century *Naturphilosophen* and Romantic Idealists, including Schelling, Goethe, and Humboldt. Most commentary has focused on the aesthetic experiences of humans regarding the structure and complexity of nature. For example, *Kunstformen der Natur* (1899–1904)[1] by the German evolutionary morphologist Ernst Haeckel was a wildly popular and influential collection of Art Deco paintings depicting the beauty of diatoms, radiolarians, jellyfish, corals, and other marine animals. The "beauty of science" tradition continues strongly today in mathematics, physics, and neuroscience.

An alternative tradition focuses on the aesthetic experiences of animals themselves. In *The Descent of Man* (1871), Charles Darwin[2] inverted the traditional relationship between human and nature by proposing that animals are, through their sexual and social choices, aesthetic agents in their own evolution. Rather than focus on human evaluations of the beauty of nature, Darwin used the plain, everyday language of human aesthetic experience to describe the sexual perceptions, judgments, and motivations of animals themselves. Thus, he described avian mating preferences as a "taste for the beautiful," or as "standards of beauty," and he described the songs of male birds as having the "power to charm" the females. Darwin described the evolutionary mechanism that results from sexual choice as *sexual selection*, which he conceived as independent and distinct from natural selection. For example, Darwin concluded that the complex display of the male Great Argus pheasant demonstrated that "the most refined beauty may serve as a sexual charm, and for no other purpose," by which he meant no *adaptive* purpose. In conclusion, Darwin thought that beauty in the natural world evolves because animals are beautiful to themselves.

In my academic work[3] and a recent book, *The Evolution of Beauty*,[4] I have expanded upon this explicitly Darwinian, aesthetic perspective on avian social evolution. Accordingly, I view mate choice as a product of the subjective experiences and aesthetic judgments of animals. I define *aesthetic evolution* as a distinct mode of evolutionary change that is an emergent consequence of sensory perception, cognitive evaluation, and choice. When animals make sexual, social, and ecological choices based on their subjective preferences—what they like—the result is the evolution of biological forms that function through the subjective experiences of other organisms.

Thus, I think that evolutionary and sensory biology provide vital intellectual contexts for empirical research in aesthetics. This discovery creates new challenges and opportunities for aesthetic philosophy, art history, and art criticism, which have long been viewed as belonging exclusively within the humanities.

In other work in aesthetic philosophy, I have expanded coevolutionary Darwinian aesthetics to encompass the aesthetic productions of both humans and nonhuman animals.[5] In brief, I have proposed that *art is a form of communication that coevolves with its evaluation.* Here, coevolution means that the form of aesthetic expression and aesthetic evaluation have mutually shaped one another through a series of interactions over time.

Before turning to questions of ornament and architecture, I would like to flesh out a few of the implications of the coevolutionary aesthetic framework that will be useful in later discussion. First, according to this view, the aesthetic qualities are neither inherent to an artwork nor in the special quality of aesthetic perceptual experience. Rather, the quality of being art lies in the historical process of coevolutionary entrainment between aesthetic expressions and the evaluations of them.

Furthermore, this coevolutionary aesthetics is an *aesthetic philosophy of art.* Thus, there are no aesthetic experiences without a history of coevolving with art, and there is no art without aesthetic coevolution. Aesthetics does not refer merely to the conceptually flat, limited, "biological," sensory dimensions of an artwork. Rather, aesthetics encompasses *any* qualities—sensory *or* cognitive—that contribute to the evaluation of that artwork. Just as concepts of what constitutes an artwork have been transformed by innovative artworks repeatedly throughout the history of art, the history of art has required repeated transformations of what constitutes the aesthetic. Over the last one hundred and fifty years, aesthetics has broadened considerably to include many completely cognitive and cultural dimensions.

This coevolutionary definition of art also means that art and aesthetics are inherently *population phenomena*—necessarily rooted in a community of aesthetic producers and evaluators. Arthur Danto

first recognized that aesthetic populations—or Artworlds—provide
the context for the establishment, or social contrivance, of aesthetic
standards.[6] Because aesthetic coevolution can proceed by either
genetic *or* cultural mechanisms, I extend Danto's Artworlds to include
both human artworlds *and* a myriad of biotic artworlds, all of which
consist of aesthetic producers and evaluators making aesthetic expressions and coevolving aesthetic judgments.

Finally, because this philosophical framework removes human
beings from the organizing center of the discipline, coevolutionary
aesthetics is a *post-human* aesthetic philosophy. The goal is not
to devalue human aesthetic achievements or complexity, nor to pro-
pose a scientifically reductive account of human aesthetics. Rather,
I hope that placing the human arts in the broader context of the
stunning diversity of biotic artworlds will enhance our understanding
of the diversity and richness of human aesthetics. Ultimately, my
goal is to develop conceptual and intellectual tools that can be applied
broadly to extraordinary aesthetic phenomena in both biotic and
human artworlds.

The Problem of Ornament

Following in a long scientific tradition since Darwin, I have often
referred to the coevolved, aesthetic, sexual signals of birds and other
animals as *ornaments*. For example, in *The Evolution of Beauty*, I
wrote that, "Ornaments are distinct in function from other parts of
the body. They do not function solely in ecological or physiological
interactions with the physical world. Rather, sexual ornaments function
in interactions with observers—through the way in which sensory
perceptions and cognitive evaluations by other individual organisms
create a subjective experience in those organisms."[7] Yet, in the
coevolutionary aesthetic framework, the coevolved aesthetic components of the avian phenotype—plumage coloration, song, and physical
displays—are *biotic art*. Thus, in *The Evolution of Beauty*, I also wrote
that "bird songs, sexual displays, animal pollinated flowers, fruits,
and so on are *art*. . . . They are biotic arts that have emerged within
myriad biotic artworlds."[8]

So are bird songs, dances, and sexual signals ornaments or art? And
what is at stake in our use of these terms?

Not surprising to anyone who knows him, my ambiguous usage of art and ornament did not escape the attention of Professor Kent Bloomer. In May 2018, a letter from Professor Bloomer inviting me to discuss ornament landed on my desk like a summons. Having dedicated my entire professional life to my own irrational (or sub-rational?) fascination and engagement with birds, I understood imme-diately that Bloomer's lifelong exploration of ornament in architecture and sculpture would be a stimulating provocation. Our discussions inspired the following introductory exploration of the many intersec-tions of ornament, architecture, and ornithology.

Avian Ornament

The body of a living bird consists of a full complement of organis-mal parts including a beak, legs and wings, feathered skin, a skeleton, lungs, a digestive tract, a brain and nervous system, gonads for reproduction, and other internal organs. These structures fulfill innu-merable functions to further the maintenance, survival, and reproduc-tion of the individual. However, some components of avian pheno-type—the totality of the body and behavior of the individual bird—stand out from all others because they have not evolved through natural selection to further individual survival, or to support the basic mechanics or ecology of reproduction. Rather, these components of the phenotype have evolved to function through the subjective perceptions and evaluations of other individual birds to fulfill *aesthetic* functions. These traits are appropriately referred to as *ornaments*.

This concept of ornament is entirely consistent with the use of ornament in art, architecture, and design.[9] In an automobile, for exam-ple, many different grill designs may work equivalently well from an engineering perspective in providing air flow to the engine's cooling system, but the specifics of the grill created for a certain model of car is a solution to a combination of these functional requirements and additional ornamental functions. The ornamental features of grill design influence the subjective evaluations of car buyers, dealers, and "influence makers" in the automotive marketplace, which is both an economic market and an artworld.

Likewise, like the avian body, most buildings must have a stable structure with complex functional innards—beams, other structural materials, a roof, electrical wiring, communications systems, plumbing, air handling systems, etc. The building's structural features must function to further the objective requirements of the building as a place to live, eat, work, exercise, do business, worship, exhibit art, etc.

Using Bloomer's vocabulary, many avian ornaments are unambiguously *born by* other structures of the avian body. Thus, the sexually attractive colors of many birds are produced by light interacting with the plumage and skin. The avian integument functions simultaneously in thermoregulation, water repellency, flight, etc., and numerous aesthetic functions. In a concise comparison with human architectural ornaments, avian plumage color ornaments are born by the skin and plumage.

Avian Architecture

Birds extend the parallel between avian ornaments and human architecture even further. Like nearly all human societies, most species of birds are *builders*. Bird nests are constructions to house a clutch of eggs and, often, the developing chicks. The only exceptions are those birds that lay their eggs in a simple scrape on the ground, or brood parasites, like cuckoos, which lay their eggs in nests of other bird species. To build their nests, birds select nest materials from their environment, and manipulate them according to genetically inherited motor patterns to construct the nest.

Many details of nest placement, nest materials, and construction methods are under strong natural selection to protect the eggs and chicks from excessive temperature variation or rain, and to hide them from predation. These sources of natural selection have contributed greatly to the adaptive radiation in nest structure across birds.

The structure and composition of bird nests are indisputably a form of animal architecture. Like human architecture, avian architecture has ancient history; nest designs are highly consistent within species, but they have evolved and diversified among species and lineages of birds. For example, the details of the architecture of the nests of the more than three hundred species of Neotropical ovenbirds (Furnariidae) provide a rich enough constellation of features that nest architecture can be used to construct a phylogeny, or historical tree, of the entire family, which has been extensively confirmed by subsequent phylogenies based on DNA (figure 1).[10]

Bird nests are under strong natural selection for adaptive solutions to reproductive challenges. But avian nest architecture is not limited to purely practical designs with measurable physical functions. Many lineages of birds have also evolved striking aesthetic innovations in nest architecture through aesthetic sexual selection.

In some bird species, males construct the nest, or begin nest construction, before mate choice occurs. In these cases, female mate choice may be based in part upon evaluations of the potential mate's nest. As we would predict, in multiple avian lineages in which the male initiates or entirely completes nest construction, nest architecture achieves some of the most striking advances in avian architectural complexity. Thus, aesthetic sexual selection on nest construction behavior has contributed to aesthetic innovation in avian architecture.

For example, the nest of the Eurasian Penduline Tit (*Remiz pendulinus*, Remizidae) is an enclosed, fleecy orb with a narrow doorway at the top of its side. The nest is made by the male by weaving and felting fine cottony plant fibers. Likewise, the nest of the closely related Verdin (*Auriparus flaviceps*), found in deserts of western North America, is an enclosed ovoid woven from plant fibers, leaves and flower stalks. Nest construction in this family (Remizidae) is initiated by the male, and continues once females have chosen a mate. Nests of the penduline tits are more complicated in architecture and construction methods than are the open-cup nests or adopted-tree-cavity nests of their closest relatives.

In several genera of migratory wrens (*Cistothorus, Troglodytes*, and *Thryothorus*; Troglodytidae), males arrive on the breeding grounds in spring, establish breeding territories, and begin nest construction before the females arrive. Wren nests are an enclosed ball woven from pliable vegetation, stems, or interlocked sticks. Before the arrival of the females, males of these wren genera build multiple nests (as many as ten!) on their territories as a display to attract a female mate. Once the female selects a mate, they finish construction of one of the male's nests for their clutch. The enclosed vegetation nest evolved in the common ancestor of the wrens from an open-cup nest,[11] perhaps, in part, through sexual selection. It is clear, however, that the initiation of construction of many more nests than can possibly function in reproduction is a derived form of aesthetic sexual communication.

The woven, hanging, enclosed vegetation nests of weavers (Ploceidae), from Africa and Asia, are perhaps the most complexly constructed of all bird nests (figure 2).[12] The spherical nest begins with a vertically oriented ring, woven from plant fibers and hanging from the twigs of a tree or shrub. A hemispherical egg chamber is then woven to one side of the ring. Next, the front edges of the ring are extended forward to complete the egg chamber, ending with a small circular doorway. At a fine, submillimeter scale, the fibers are woven into complex and highly stable interlocking patterns and knots. Different lineages of weavers have elaborated on this basic plan to produce an extraordinary aesthetic radiation in nest architecture (figure 3). In multiple different species, the doorway is extended downward in a long hanging tube, or retort entrance. The tubular retort entrance can be either tightly or loosely woven, or it can hang free or be incorporated into the body of the egg chamber. The Sociable Weaver (*Philetairus socius*) species builds a massive stick apartment house which can be five meters across and include dozens, to over a hundred separate egg chambers used by different pairs.

Like penduline tits and many wrens, weaver nests are constructed entirely by the male prior to pair formation. Some weavers are also colonial, with many dozens of nests in a single tree. In some species, males are polygynous, and a particularly attractive male may have multiple mates raising different broods in various nests. It appears that sexual selection on the male *and* his nest has resulted in multiple architectural innovations, including egg chamber elaboration from a vertical ring, complex weaving, and the retort entrance. These are all likely to be aesthetic innovations in avian architecture.

Many species of birds conspicuously ornament the egg chamber or outer surfaces of their nests with nonstructural materials that appear to function in communication. For example, the Firewood-gatherer (*Anumbius anumbi*, Furnariidae) is a small, forty-five-gram ovenbird from open country in southern South America. The male and female pair construct an enormous, enclosed stick nest that may be two to three feet in diameter. The doorway and the top surface of the nest are conspicuously ornamented with very unusual and specific objects collected from the environment, including bleached bones, small animal skulls, shed snake and lizard skins, large feathers from other bird species, owl pellets, pieces of fur, mammal scat, and even human trash. Male and female Firewood-gatherers are identical in appearance, but recent research on pairs that have been sexed genetically demonstrates that only the male gathers and incorporates these ornamental materials to adorn the surface of the nest.[13] What is the function of these somewhat morbid or gruesome ornaments? That is still unknown. They could be warnings or revolting signals to potential predators. However, selection for such a signal would not likely be sex-limited. Thus, this unusual nest ornamentation behavior appears to have evolved by sexual selection.

No discussion of avian architecture would be complete without mentioning the most fantastical avian architects—the bowerbirds (Ptilonorhynchidae) of Australia and New Guinea. Male bowerbirds construct bowers, and ornament them with a bizarre variety of natural objects gathered from the environment. The bower is not a nest, but a "seduction theater" that the male uses to court potential mates.[14] Females visit various males at their bowers, select a mate, and raise the offspring by themselves in a simple open-cup nest of their own construction. Males build a complex bower as a stage on which to display to visiting females.

The complexity and diversity of bower structure and design establishes, beyond doubt, that they constitute animal architecture.[15] There are two main classes of bower structure. Avenue bowers feature a pair of parallel walls with a narrow passageway between them for the female to sit (figure 4) and observe the male's display. The ground in front of one opening is decorated with selected materials. Maypole bowers feature a central sapling supporting a "bottlebrush"-shaped pile of sticks, surrounded by a mossy circular runway, or moat, around it (figure 5). The ornamental features can cover the central twigs or the mossy runway. Although the courtship behavior of bowerbirds is too complex and diverse to adequately review here, current research indicates that the bower has a combination of aesthetic, architectural, and social features. The materials gathered for display are extremely idiosyncratic, specific, and variable among species: all blue items, all white items, or always snail shells. Furthermore, there are additional variations in architecture within avenue and maypole bowers.

Ornaments or Art?

The richness and diversity of avian aesthetics presents other examples that do not fit neatly into the concept of ornament. If an aesthetic trait is performed by an individual—such as a bird song or a courtship display—then these performances cannot be appropriately viewed as grounded in the utilitarian, or non-aesthetic, functions of the bird.

In dance, music, sculpture, or painting, a narrow concept of ornament as *born by* underlying structural elements conflicts with a similar account of ornament in architecture because the underlying "structural elements" in these artworks are themselves aesthetic in function. The structural elements of a symphony, sculpture, or painting have no objective functions outside of their coevolved aesthetic functions.

For example, the green patina of the copper roof or gutters of a building can be analyzed effectively as ornaments *born by* underlying functional structures of the building. But the bright rusty color of the monumental steel sculptures, *Torqued Ellipses*, by Richard Serra are not *born by* the massive, undulating pieces of steel in the same way, because the steel has no non-aesthetic functions. The physical process—oxidation of the exposed surface of a metal alloy—is identical, yet the distinction of the ornamental is not clear.

This distinction is even more complex in human performance arts. An entire dance or vocal performance can be seen as being *born by* the body of the human performer. But this gives rise to two new complexities. First, the human body itself is a complex of objective adaptations—grasping hands with opposing thumbs, vocal cords and resonant buccal cavity for speech—and aesthetic features—permanent female breast tissue; scalp, armpit, and pubic hair—that have evolved through sexual or social selection.[16] Furthermore, in the performing arts, ornament is traditionally viewed as a limited or superficial detail of the performance, like a momentary gesture of a dancer's hand or a brief jazz improvisation within a broader structure of chord progression.

I think this conception of ornament from fine arts—as a superficial and spatio-temporally restricted detail of a broader aesthetic structure—contributes to the denigration of ornament as insubstantial and unimportant, and to the decline of ornament in the arts. In short, avian aesthetic diversity cannot be entirely captured by the concept of ornament that works so well within the field of architecture.

My solution to this conundrum has been to recognize performances, and all their details, as products of aesthetic coevolution. Thus, like a human dance, a song, a poem, or novel, an entire avian aesthetic performance can best be considered as an artwork that coevolves with aesthetic evaluation. We do not imagine that ballets, operas, or novels are aesthetic ornaments of human beings that create them, but full artworks performed or created by them. Likewise, many of the aesthetic entities produced in biotic artworlds should be conceived of as independent artworks, rather than as ornaments. In conclusion, I think we need two comparative terms—biotic ornaments and biotic artworks—to handle the ontological complexity of biotic art.

References to biotic artworks do not mean abandoning the concept of biotic ornament. Quite the contrary, I hope that the application of this broader coevolutionary aesthetic framework will energize research into ornament in architecture and the human arts.

Commonalities of Evolutionary Biology and Human Aesthetic Culture

Kent Bloomer's provocation to think more clearly about ornament has inspired a few intellectual provocations of my own. I want to highlight certain intellectual parallels between twentieth-century evolutionary biology and aesthetic culture in architecture, design, the arts, and the humanities. In particular, I would like to trace some of the common footprints left by the march of modernism in both science and the arts.

The Tyranny of Big Ideas: In the twentieth century, both evolutionary biology and architecture were subjected to a Tyranny of Big Ideas. Evolutionary biology has long been dominated by "adaptationism"— the idea that adaptation by natural selection is a strong, deterministic force that drives all of the important details of evolutionary process. In parallel, twentieth-century architecture has been dominated by the idea that modernity necessitates a certain style of intellectual progress involving the triumph of space, line, and materiality unobscured by ornament or detail. (Of course, I think that each of these Big Ideas involve fascinating, important, legitimate, and innovative implications.

My complaint is not with ideas, but with the intellectual tyrannies waged in their name).

Over the twentieth century, these independent intellectual currents in evolutionary biology, architecture, and the arts contributed to the denigration and diminishment of ornament and any interest in it. In evolutionary biology, sexual and social ornaments were explained away as adaptive signals of the objective mate quality or of species identity. In other words, ornaments and the preferences for them were explained as just another form of adaptive improvement. The result was to *explain away* ornament as a rational utility to achieve the universal goal of material betterment, rather than explain it as a product and consequence of animal subjectivity. Like many tyrannies, this framework was packaged as a new intellectual "synthesis" of formerly disparate phenomena, but the real goal of such "synthesis" was to define out of existence any intellectual interest in the function of ornament itself—ornament for its own sake. The goal was to police the boundaries of science, quash the legitimately Darwinian concern for animal subjectivity, and celebrate the triumph of the adaptationist view.

In architecture and other arts, Modernist movements embraced the narrative of disciplinary progress through intellectual and visual purity, which sought to shed ornament and recast it as historically dated, quaint, or even politically retrograde.

A Regard for History: In his book about political discourse in post-Soviet Russia and the United States, *The Road to Unfreedom,* Yale University historian Timothy Snyder describes how a Tyranny of Big Ideas can create a *politics of inevitability*—the notion that history itself is inevitably moving *forward,* progressing towards a deterministic end point.[17] Regardless of whether Big Ideas are scientific, political, cultural, or aesthetic, the politics of inevitability erases the importance of history itself, and contributes to the denigration of intellectual analyses of the contingency and individuality of history itself.

This dynamic has played out in similar ways in the disciplines of evolutionary biology and architecture. In evolutionary biology, adaptationism implies that evolutionary history and homology are unimportant residua of adaptive progress. According to this view, if one were to replay the History of Life over again from the beginning, the results

would be something familiar and highly similar to the organic world
we have today. This ahistorical view of evolution had real intellectual
consequences. For example, the leaders of the twentieth-century
"New Synthesis" in evolutionary biology opposed, and fought against,
the development and application of phylogenetic methods to investi-
gate the Tree of Life.[18]

Likewise, in architecture and the arts, Modernism viewed aesthetic
history as simply a long, groping preamble to the contemporary
emergence of a new conceptual clarity and functional purity in the
arts that would become devoid of ornament and expunge all primitive, aesthetic elements.

As Snyder concludes in his analysis of political change in the
twenty-first century, the best inoculation from the Tyranny of Big Ideas
is a deep intellectual engagement with history—a respect for individuality and contingency of history itself. Thus, a sincere intellectual
interest in ornament leads one necessarily to an engagement with
its variety, diversity, and history. Thus, just as Bloomer has engaged
in the deep history of the *Acanthus* leaf motif and the foliated scroll
in Western architecture,[19] my own research has been engaged with
phylogenetic analysis of the origin and differentiation of the courtship
displays of the species of Neotropical manakins (Pipridae).[20] The goal
of both methods and analyses are the investigation of the individuality
of each historical instance of ornament and their transformations over
time, and the discovery of generalizations that can be made from
historical patterns of aesthetic innovation, modification, and radiation.

Decoration and Decorum: In the *Nature of Ornament,* Bloomer
documents that the word *decoration* shares linguistic roots with
decorum. Thus, decoration refers not only to aesthetic embellishment,
but to the social context in which these embellishments are observed,
evaluated, and function. This concept of ornament as framed by the
broader social context of aesthetic evaluation is also captured by
coevolutionary aesthetic theory, in which all aesthetic questions are
understood within the artworlds in which interacting signalers and
receivers interact. Sexual and social context are necessary to any
investigation of aesthetic evolution in nature, and thus reinforce the
concept of decoration as decorum.

The Beauty Problem: With all of the intellectual pressure against it, why has ornament and the interest in it continued to survive and even thrive? Despite its persistent untrendiness, why does beauty endure?

In coevolutionary aesthetics, the aesthetic properties—aesthetic qualities like beauty, cuteness, irony, pathos, etc.—arise as a result of evaluations that occur within specific social interactions within an artworld. For example, whether a specific combination of colors is sexually attractive or powerfully frightening will depend critically on the artworld in which these aesthetic expressions evolve. The red, orange, and black patterns of the Channel-billed Toucan (*Ramphastos vitellinus ariel*) and the Eastern Coral Snake (*Micrurus fulvius*) are similar in hue, and both would be considered boldly attractive to most human viewers.

In the artworld of the toucan, these colors create a socially and sexually attractive combination of stimuli. However, the same combination of hues creates a coevolving genre of horror in the artworld of the coral snake and birds that could prey upon them—including toucans. The snake's bold colors are advertising its venomous threat to avian survival, to dissuade avian predators from even trying to eat it. This shows that nature doesn't just do beauty. Rather, the aesthetic properties of an aesthetic entity are not determined strictly by its material properties or the sensory impressions it creates, but by the specific social context of the artworld within which it has coevolved.

This comparison also illustrates another important property of beauty. Beauty invites, or even demands, prolonged social and sensory engagement, but aesthetic revulsion does not. As a consequence, in biotic artworlds, beauty can evolve greater diversity and complexity than revulsion because it functions to maintain the attention of the evaluator. Longer engagement with an artwork creates greater opportunity for more elaborate and detailed evaluation. Thus, beauty itself begets diversity and complexity. Similarly, in architecture and human art, aesthetic properties that are purely conceptual or cognitive—like mathematical relationships within minimalist music or opaque concepts about the meaning of line or space—create more and more barriers to direct sensory engagement, less and less purely sensory reward for the viewer. This is the reason that modern art alienates many nonexperts. Because sensory delight continues to broadly engage the viewer in the most direct and ongoing manner, beauty fosters the aesthetic engagement that fuels coevolutionary processes. In contrast, aesthetic concepts may stimulate thought, but they do not necessarily demand continued engagement from the viewer. No matter how revolutionary it was at the time, on repeated viewing Duchamp's *Fountain* simply becomes a flipped-over urinal.

Consequently, beauty endures, and will always survive, because it is the most fundamental aesthetic property of all—it is the most immediate mode of aesthetic response. Of course, this does *not* mean that beauty is universal or lawlike. It is clear from the history of human art, as it is from ornithology, that *what* is beautiful is unstable and continues to coevolve. Yet, its essential role in engaging the observer in the most immediate and direct manner means that beauty—and its decorous agent, ornament—will always find its place in nature and the human arts.

The Big Difference: Ornithologists are students of avian diversity, its evolutionary history, and the mechanisms that have fostered it. We are in the influence business. We try to influence how others *think* about birds, evolution, and ecology, and hopefully conserve them. But we are not in the business of creating new birds. We hope that our ideas take flight, but we don't imagine that they will someday actually bear feathers. We educate students, but we do not to prepare them to go into the world to create new birds. In short, ornithologists are stuck with the birds we've got.

In contrast, architecture has one foot in the history of architectural form and diversity, and another in its creation and innovation. Architects put theory and ideas into action through the creation of new structures and spaces. They also educate new generations of practitioners to continue this ancient tradition in newly relevant and creative ways. As a scientist, I can only envy them for their new birds.

Notes

1. Ernst Heinrich Philipp August Haeckel, *Kunstformen Der Natur*, 2 vols. (Leipzig, Wien: Verlag des Bibliographischen Instituts, 1899).

2. Charles Darwin, *The Descent of Man, and Selection in Relation to Sex*, 2 vols. (London: John Murray, Albemarle Street, 1871).

3. Patricia L.R. Brennan and Richard O. Prum, "The limits of sexual conflict in the narrow sense: new insights from waterfowl biology," *Philosophical transactions of the Royal Society of London* B 367 (2012): 2324–338; Prum, "Phylogenetic tests of alternative intersexual selection mechanisms: macroevolution of male traits in a polygynous clade (Aves: Pipridae)," *American Naturalist,* 149 (1997): 668–92; Prum, "The Lande-Kirkpatrick mechanism is the null model of evolution by intersexual selection: implications for meaning, honesty, and design in intersexual signals," *Evolution* 64 (2010): 3085–100; Prum, "Aesthetic evolution by mate choice: Darwin's *really* dangerous idea," *Philosophical transactions of the Royal Society of London* B 367 (2012): 2253–265.

4. Prum, *The Evolution of Beauty: How Darwin's Forgotten Theory of Mate Choice Shapes the Animal World—and Us* (New York: Doubleday, 2017), 448.

5. Prum, "Coevolutionary aesthetics in human and biotic artworlds," *Biology and Philosophy* 28 (2013): 811–32.

6. A.C. Danto, "The Artworld," *Journal of Philosophy* 61 (1964): 571–84.

7. Prum, *The Evolution of Beauty*, 6–7.

8. Ibid. 336.

9. Kent Bloomer, *The Nature of Ornament: Rhythm and Metamorphosis in Architecture*, first edition (New York: W.W. Norton, 2000), 250.

10. Krzysztof Zyskowski and Richard O. Prum, "Phylogenetic analysis of nest architecture of the Neotropical ovenbirds (Furnariidae)" in *Auk* 116 (1999): 891–911.

11. Carl H. Oliveros, et al., "Earth history and the passerine superradiation," *Proceedings of the National Academy of Sciences* 116 (16) (2019): 7916. The sister group to the wrens is the gnatwens (Polioptilidae) which build a small open-cup nest of fine vegetation fibers, spider webs, and lichens.

12. Nicholas E. Collias and Elsie C. Collias, *Nest Building and Bird Behavior* (Princeton: Princeton University Press, 1984).

13. Kaspar Delhey, et al., "Complex nest decorations of a small brown bird in the Pampas," *Frontiers in Ecology and the Environment* 15 (2017): 406–07.

14. Prum, *The Evolution of Beauty*.

15. Ibid.

16. Ibid.

17. Timothy Snyder, *The Road to Unfreedom: Russia, Europe, America*, first edition (New York: Tim Duggan Books, 2018), 368.

18. David L. Hull, *Science as a Process: An Evolutionary Account of the Social and Conceptual Development of Science*, Science and Its Conceptual Foundations series (Chicago: University of Chicago Press, 1988).

19. Bloomer, *The Nature of Ornament: Rhythm and Metamorphosis in Architecture*, first edition (New York: W.W. Norton, 2000).

20. Prum, "Phylogenetic analysis of the evolution of display behavior in the Neotropical manakins (Aves: Pipridae)," *Ethology* 84 (1990): 202–31; see also Prum, "Phylogenetic tests ofalternative intersexual selection mechanisms": 668–92; Prum, *The Evolution of Beauty.*

21. Zyskowski and Prum, "Phylogenetic analysis of nest architecture": 891–911.

22. Ibid.

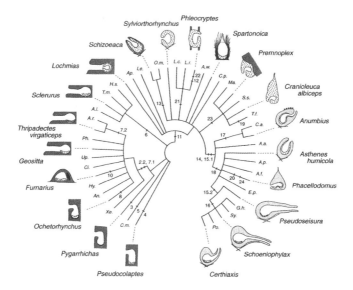

1. A phylogenetic tree of the Neotropical ovenbirds (Furnariidae) based on characters of nest structure, material composition, and construction methods from K. Zyskowski and R. Prum, "Phylogenetic analysis of nest architecture of the Neotropical ovenbirds (Furnariidae)" in Auk 116 (1999): 891–911. The nest architecture of ovenbirds has evolved from a single nest type in the original common ancestor to a tremendous variety of nests, all of which feature an enclosed egg chamber.

2. Male weavers (Ploceidae) construct their nests by weaving plant fibers in a characteristic series of stages, shown here for the Village Weaver (Ploceus cucullatus). Top left: Stage 1– construction of a woven ring; top center: Stage 2–extension of the egg chamber from the top of the back of the ring; top right: Stage 3–completion of the egg chamber; bottom left: Stage 4–forward extension of the entrance top of the front of the ring; and bottom right: Stage 5– completion of the entrance. Illustration by Michael DiGiorgio.

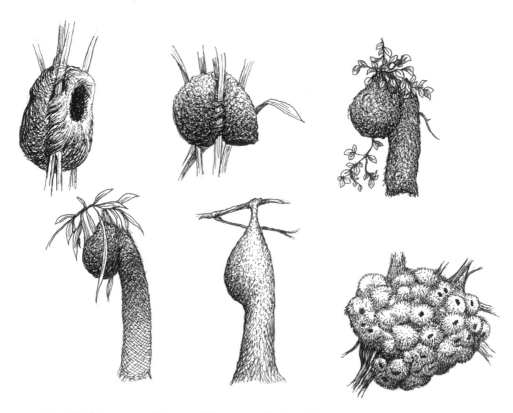

3. Top left: Thick-billed Weaver (Amblyospiza albifrons) nest with a forward-facing entrance above the level of the egg chamber; top center: Orange Weaver (Ploceus aurantius) nest with a downward-facing entrance at the level of the egg chamber; top right: Black-necked Weaver (Ploceus nigricollis) nest with a long, tightly woven, retort entrance tunnel; bottom left: Red-vented Malimbe (Malimbus scutatus) nest with a long, open weave, transparent, retort entrance tunnel; bottom center: Baya Weaver (Ploceus phillippinus) nest with a long, tightly woven, retort entrance tunnel incorporated into the egg chamber; and bottom right: Sociable Weaver (Philetairus socius) colonial nest with dozens of separate entrances to different egg chambers. Illustration by Michael DiGiorgio.

4. An avenue bower of the Great Bowerbird (Chlamydera nuchalis) from Broome, Western Australia. The male has decorated the front of the bower with a pile of hundreds of fossil shells from a stratum in a cliff face over the ocean a couple of kilometers away. Photograph by Richard O. Prum.

5. A maypole bower of MacGregor's Bowerbird (Amblyornis macgregoriae) from Papua New Guinea. Photograph by Brett Benz.

KALEIDOSCOPE/ COLLIDE-I-SCOPE: ORNAMENT AS MANTRA AND MANDALA AT GURU NANAK DWARA

Guru Dev Khalsa

Guru Dev Khalsa is a Yale School of Architecture graduate and collaborated with Kent Bloomer on the installation of a legacy ornament for the Sikh community of Guru Nanak Dwara in Phoenix, Arizona.

My phone vibrated with an incoming call from Professor Kent Bloomer. *I* inquired how the hammering was going. *He* invited me to present our collaboration on Guru Nanak Dwara in honor of his retirement from Yale—I must admit to initial uncertainty. Having left conventional academia upon graduating from the School of Architecture in 2004, I felt rather unqualified. In fact, a lingering sense of guilt remained about an anemic paper I'd submitted on Sikh architecture for an independent study under Kent's mentorship in my final year. Is that what this was about, I thought? Karmic payback? After fifteen years, the satisfaction of his retirement hung on *my* ability to deliver a decent paper? But when I voiced my concern, Kent left me with advice I will never forget. Like a true champion of the underdog—a man who finds magic in all things—he said to me: "Just be Guru Dev."

The presentation has come and gone. I was nervous, but everyone at Yale had been gracious. Synchronizing 143 slides and four minutes of video to a half-written, half-improvised speech, I had attempted to present life at Guru Nanak Dwara in the best "Guru Dev way" I could. But I have struggled to commit these final words to paper.

Like an ever-shifting kaleidoscope, my thoughts converge and reflect upon the fundamental truth that Kent's work simply cannot be expressed in the static finality of cold, hard print. I stare at the black and white of my screen, scrolling through the word bank of a neglected vocabulary, but the dictionary is of no assistance in imparting the poetry of how it is to live in the ornament of Kent Bloomer. How can I describe the choreography of light when it dances through an arabesque? How can I convey the sacred sounds that fill this chamber of devotion, animating every form with spiritual vibration? These forms that were conceived in the imaginations of dear friends . . . scratched out in pen and paper, studying every line and taper, carved and molded by sinews of dedication and love that guided every stroke, every cut, every grasp and compression, every caress . . . to bring an idea to life. How can I?

The saints and sages, the Gurus, whose verses are contained in the sacred scriptures of the Sikhs, repeatedly ask this question. And yet they have dedicated one thousand, four hundred and thirty pages of poetry to this very effort.

I have only one tongue — which of Your Glorious Virtues
can I describe?
Unlimited, infinite Lord and Master — no one knows your limits.
—SGGS Ang: 674 Sri Guru Arjan Dev Ji

And so, I too endeavor, in the best Guru Dev way I can, to share
what has revealed itself to me through many meditations in and upon,
through and beyond, the design and ornament that unifies Guru Nanak
Dwara as a place where the sacred permeates every moment and
interstice. It is a place that has evolved over time—decades, in fact.
And many people have been involved along the way. I often say that
Guru Nanak Dwara has a life of its own, and so it is with all creative
efforts. For the Divine Doer is our constant companion, and I bow to
the wondrous flow of the Creator in Creation.

Long ago, the mirror of truth was shattered into innumerable
pieces, leaving us each with a shard to recognize truth in the eyes
of our own reflection. But what if we created a relationship to hold
the fractured pieces together, so that we began to see ourselves in
the myriad fragments of truth held in the name of another? What
if we formed ourselves into a kaleidoscope (figure 1)?

We know that the effect of a kaleidoscope is achieved by angling
reflectors towards one another, such that repeated symmetrical
patterns are revealed. The Greek root words define it as the observation of beautiful forms. *Kalos* means beauty. Beauty inspires joy and
love. *Eidos* is that which is seen, perceived by the eye, the eye being
a window to the soul. *Scopeo* is to look to, to examine, to observe,
which is to allow for an experience.

It is interesting that symmetry is a factor in the creation of this
concept of beauty, so let us also define symmetry. *Symmetry* is a balance of proportions, a one-to-one correspondence of parts on
opposite sides. But let us not approach symmetry superficially, and
rather understand it as being achieved by the balance of recognizing
ourselves in the other, an unshakeable trust that all creation is the
equal and infinite expression of the Divine.

So, if we gather all of our reflectors, our eyes, these viewers and
perceivers that inform our views and perceptions, and align them at

symmetrical angles, to become angels, we will experience the beauty of allowing love to enter the gates of the soul.

This was the practice of Guru Nanak, who did not set out to create the religion of Sikhs, but rather to awaken the infinite forms of Creation in Unity with the One Creator. This was the life of Yogi Bhajan, who, five hundred years later, left India and crossed the *terrifying world ocean* to deliver Guru Nanak's message to the West: "If you can't see God in All," he said, "you can't see God at all." And with that he created "3HO," the Healthy, Happy, Holy Organization.

Yogi Bhajan was extremely fond of creating homophones. In his honor, we will translate the word kaleidoscope into the three words *collide*, *I*, and *scope*. To *collide* is to impact, *I*, my sense of individual self, in the *scope*, a space or opportunity for unhampered activity or thought.

If we ask *why* should we do this? Treat yourself to the sight of a young child meditating in the purity of their own innocence, and I dare you to question any further. Then we are left with *where*, and *how* do we achieve this kaleidoscopic effect, this opportunity to impact our sense of individualization towards an experience of oneness?

One such *where* is found in a *Gurdwara*, which means gate to the Guru. *Gu* means darkness. *Ru* means light. The Guru is the *paaras*, or philosopher's stone, which transforms darkness to light, dispelling the painful illusion of separation to awaken the bliss of oneness. A Gurdwara is therefore a portal to access the Guru, the philosopher's stone, to transform the finite self and merge with the infinite.

How we do this, as taught by Guru Nanak and Yogi Bhajan, is through the vibration of the recitation of the divine sound current. Our bodies are seventy percent water. The vibrations we create and receive ripple through our entire being. When Yoga, the yoke of a spiritual practice, is donned, with a devotional longing for reunification, then meditation, with mantra, with simran, with *Naam Jaap*, replaces the obstacles of the mind, rewrites the narrative of the subconscious, and transforms the lens, the filters, and the framework of our perceptions, to realign our perspective so that we might recognize divinity in all and gain a true experience of ourselves. This is the kaleidoscope of divine alchemy.

Guru Nanak Dwara, a Sikh Gurdwara founded by Yogi Bhajan, is dedicated to the mission of unity, and to the practices by which to achieve it. Just as the Guru is the alchemist of humanity, ornament is the alchemy of architecture and transforms the mundane and earthly into something sacred. To paraphrase Professor Bloomer, ornament makes visible the motions of the universe by pulling them into the realm of the Earth for all to see. The architecture and ornament of this Gurdwara create a mandala that expresses the three worlds, or realms, described in the Sikh scriptures, and symbolizes Guru Nanak's journey to oneness with the infinite and his message of unity and equality for all creation. His story goes like this:

> Each day before sunrise, Guru Nanak went to the river to bathe in the cold water and sing God's praises. But one day, he disappeared into the river and could not be found. Three days later, he emerged having had a powerful vision of the nature of reality, divinity, and human existence. He described the experience of this moment of enlightenment in the song known as *Japji Sahib*—the "Song of the Soul." It begins like this:

> *"Ek Ong Kaar, Sat Naam, Kartaa Purakh, Nirbhao, Nirvair, Akaal Moorat, Ajoonee, Saibhang, Gurprasaad, Jap. Aad Sach, Jugaad Sach, Haibee Sach, Naanak Hosee Bhee Sach!"*

> *One Creator. Truth is His name. Doer of everything. Without Fear, Without Revenge, Undying, Unborn, Self-illumined. The Guru's gift, Meditate! True in the beginning. True through all the ages. True even now. Oh Nanak it is forever true.*

Guru Nanak set forth from that day, traveling many miles by foot, to promote the message of equality and oneness. He taught that the best way to achieve this experience was through the vibration of the recitation of God's Name.

Like the mandalas of many Indian religions, the parti diagram of Guru Nanak Dwara is a basic square form with a large central space, a tower at each corner and four gates—or doors, rather—that open to the four directions. The mandala represents a place of community and connection in support of meditation. The four doors greet people from all walks of life. The perimeter of Guru Nanak Dwara is open and welcoming, intended to invite interaction. There is a continuous marble walkway surrounding the Gurdwara which enhances the meditative practice of circumambulating barefoot around the complex. The colors and patterns of the marble design allude to rippling water, and to the beautiful lotus blossom that grows out of the muck to float serenely on top. The lotus is a reminder that from the challenges of daily life we must rise to our highest self (figure 2).

The lotus symbol is repeated in the railing surrounding the sunken courtyard, which has marble patterns that continue the theme above. The railing also contains geometric patterns representing the mandala and parti diagram of the Gurdwara, establishing a rhythm similar to the cadence of one who might circumambulate in meditation (figures 3–4).

The inner sanctuary of Guru Nanak Dwara is an homage to Guru Nanak's enlightenment in the river. The ornament and design unify the environment to illustrate this narrative and express the sacred for the purposes of meditation and devotional worship. Each individual enters with their own narrative, but like water in water, by chanting and meditating, the individual merges in unity with the divine sound current.

The hall also represents the three worlds: the surface realm of the earth, the trees and sky above, and the dirt and water below. We start below with the blue carpet, which represents the river (figure 5). Many passages in the sacred scriptures of the Sikhs also refer to the *terrifying world ocean*. This is a metaphor for *maya*, which is the illusion, distraction, and attachment that keep us from remembering our true, divine nature. Immersion in the vibration of the sacred music helps us cross the world ocean of *maya* and awaken to the realization of *Ek Ong Kar*, that the Creator and Creation are One, that we all come from the same energy, and are all equal. The pinwheel patterns in the carpet represent the rafts of devotional recitation that will carry us across the world ocean. They rotate away from the center aisle, like the parting of the ocean on the path to truth. At the end of the aisle, we bow as an act of surrendering the ego to the higher unknown power of the Infinite. This is a great practice for when our hearts and minds are heavy.

Kent Bloomer Studio is designing pilasters that will evoke Guru Nanak's watery submersion. Lotus blossom fixtures will rise out of the murky mud through water that becomes clearer and clearer, to inspire us with the beauty that grows out of life's hardships and challenges. When the lotus blossom of the crown chakra, the tenth gate at the top of the head, opens through meditative practice, nectar pours in and one gains an experience of enlightenment (figure 6).

The lotus figure continues in the railing that runs around the mezzanine. It is shown both in elevation at a youthful state and in plan at a fully mature state. Between the blossoms are medallions that have been abstracted from the Gurmukhi characters of *Ek Ong Kar*. Despite the tumultuousness of life, we are reminded to connect with our highest self and come through as bright and as beautiful as the lotus blossom with an experience of unity with all. This is the middle realm of the surface of the earth on which humanity dwells.

The Sanctuary Hall is enclosed by scalloped arches that articulate the dome and canopy of the sky. The Bloomer Studio is fabricating ceiling tiles sculpted in the geometry of an octagonal interlace with gold-tipped edges, to shine like the stars in an infinite cycle without beginning or end. This completes the three realms.

Just like a mandala, the ornament not only creates a narrative but also serves in meditation. Ornament is to form what *mantra* is to sound. *Mantra* is the creative projection of the mind through sound. *Man* is the mind. *Trang* means wave or projection. The pattern, combination, meaning, rhythmical repetition and punctuation of specific words or sounds help to focus concentration in meditation and elevate consciousness. Similarly, the pattern, combination, meaning, rhythmical repetition and punctuation of form in ornament is like a visual mantra, creating new narratives and pathways in the mind to alter our perception and realign our perspective towards an experience of oneness. In this way, the ornament at Guru Nanak Dwara, like the people who enter, are all jewels in the kaleidoscope of Divine alchemy that reflects the treasure of spiritual wisdom (figure 7).

At this point, you may still be wondering what Kent was hammering when I picked up the phone those many moons ago, and I will keep you in the dark no longer. The latest Bloomer project to arrive at Guru Nanak Dwara is an installation of sixteen lotus luminaires that will float about the perimeter of the Gurdwara to illuminate nighttime ambulation. Each luminaire contains twenty leaves lovingly hammered into form by Kent himself. The mantra of his life force will echo the unstruck sound in a protective and projective ring around the Gurdwara (figure 8).

The luminaire is itself divided into the three realms, with the lotus on the surface, the reflected petals below, and the stamen rising above. The surface of the water is expressed by a plate that has been cut into the lacy geometry of concentric ripples like the vibration of the divine sound current rippling through our bodies. This defining moment of transition between the earth and the realm below is a very exciting zone of study. The railings of both the inner sanctuary and the outer courtyard have a similar moment to be explored and will likely house ornament that incorporates the sacred script of the *Gurbani*, the Guru's word. For it is by instruction of the Guru, the *paraas* or philosopher's stone, that we are led to produce the sound current of meditation to blossom the lotus of the tenth gate and receive the blissful nectar of Divine union. It is this magical moment of transition, this slip between one side and the other, where the alchemy of ornament resides, and we are given a glimpse of the motions of the universe.

The final *puari*, or step, of *Japji Sahib* uses the metaphor of the goldsmith to describe the path to Oneness:

> Let self-control be the furnace, and patience the goldsmith.
> Let understanding be the anvil, and spiritual wisdom the tools.
> Let the surrender to God be the bellows and fan the flames of the inner life force.
> In the crucible of love, melt the nectar of the Name,
> And mint the coin of the Word of God.
> Such is the karma of those upon whom He has cast His glance of Grace.
> O Nanak, the Merciful Lord, by His Grace, uplifts and exalts them.

Professor Bloomer is one of the most fascinating people in my life. His purpose is to create a magical beauty that transforms ordinary structures into exalted environments. Like the patient goldsmith he has spanned the decades with his legacy of ornament. But even greater than that is his role as a teacher and a mentor to so many seekers who are touched by the *paraas* of his enthusiasm and love for life, and are transformed in the alchemy of his ability to illuminate the truth of their best self. *Lux et Veritas.*

And now I must give thanks to my parents, Jodha Singh and Gurukirn Kaur, who never gave up, and have committed their lives and earnings to see Guru Nanak Dwara, and me, transformed by the alchemy of Professor Bloomer and his ornament, to become the best we can be.

1. *Kaleidoscopic view*, Guru Nanak Dwara. Photograph by Jessie Peña, AZ Home Drone, 2019.

2. *Elevations*, Guru Nanak Dwara. Drawings courtesy Kent Bloomer Studio, 2006.

3. *Railing with Lotus Symbol,* Guru Nanak Dwara. Photograph by Michael Jennings Photography, 2019.

4. *Railing with Lotus Symbol,* Guru Nanak Dwara. Photograph by Michael Jennings Photography, 2019.

5. *Inner Sanctuary*, Guru Nanak Dwara. Photograph by Michael Jennings Photography, 2019.

6. *Mezzanine*, Guru Nanak Dwara. Photograph by Michael Jennings Photography, 2019.

7. Top and bottom: *Railing Detail*, Guru Nanak Dwara. Photograph by Michael Jennings Photography, 2019.

8. *Luminaire*, Guru Nanak Dwara. Photograph by Michael Jennings Photography, 2019.

9. *Luminaire*, Guru Nanak Dwara. Photograph by Michael Jénnings Photography, 2019.

CHARLIE "YARDBIRD" PARKER AND THE WILD BLUE YONDER: A PLANETARIUM FOR THE EAR BASED ON JOHANNES KEPLER'S 1619 HARMONICES MUNDI

Willie Ruff

Willie Ruff is a jazz musician and retired Professor of Music from Yale University. He founded the Duke Ellington Fellowship at Yale in 1972.

Kent Bloomer and I share some peculiarities that only come to two drummers at an early age: an obsession with rhythm that makes us crazy in a way that is divine. In the 1970s, when I taught an interdisciplinary seminar at the Yale School of Music on the subject of rhythm, everybody told me that I had to meet Kent. I became so drawn to Kent's work in rhythm that I had him address my graduate seminar at the School of Music called the Yale Interdisciplinary Seminar on Rhythm. We walked around the campus with Kent looking at rhythmic expressions of architecture throughout the courtyards and stone buildings. We became friends, and I would go and address his students about rhythm as well.

That all occurred some decades after Charlie Parker stepped into my life, which was at a very particular moment: while I was still with the Tuskegee Airmen, wearing that very sharp uniform. We were 1,400 black airmen at Lockbourne Air Force Base outside of Columbus, Ohio. In 1948, President Truman signed an executive order to integrate all of the American Armed Forces a year hence. By 1949, we had begun the process and that air base was going to be closed down. I happened to pick up a jazz magazine called *Downbeat Magazine*, and in it was an interview with Charlie Parker, my hero, the high priest of modern Jazz. He was the master ornamenter and improvizer. The person conducting the interview asked,

> "Bird, Yard Bird, if you could do with the next several years of your life whatever you wanted to do, what would it be?"

> He said, "Oh, that's an easy question. I've gone as far as I could have gone alone [in] my own musical study. I need more formal training. If I had my druthers, I would go to New Haven, where this fabulous composer Paul Hindemith is teaching music theory and composition, and I would sit at his feet and learn me some music."

I knew very little about Paul Hindemith, and I had no idea that Yale had that kind of musical distinction, or that Bird thought that much on this cat. So, I applied, wrote away for a catalog, and they invited me to come to this campus in my little soldier suit. At seventeen, I thought I was sharp. And, by some miracle, they let me in. Charlie Parker never showed up, which broke my heart—I thought that if I was working there with this cat he so much admired and him too, that I would be in heaven's heaven working with them both. And then I learned that Charlie Parker would have been surprised—not disappointed, but surprised—at what Hindemith had on his mind. It wasn't the kind of thing that you would expect from what Hindemith was composing at the time. The man was obsessed with the life of Johannes Kepler! He was writing his most ambitious work, a huge opera, about the life of Johannes Kepler, who lived before, during, and after the Thirty Years' War, in the late 1500s to early 1600s. And in this treatise, Hindemith had found all aspects of Kepler's life to be of great personal importance: Hindemith was also a German like Kepler, and like Kepler, had to flee his native Germany. Hitler ran him out, and so in 1940, Hindemith emigrated to the United States and ended up on the faculty of the Yale School of Music. So, I entered Hindemith's classes and found him covering the blackboard with all of these mathematical equations of Kepler's three laws of planetary motion.

Hindemith was writing an opera on Kepler's life at this time, and found in him a kindred spirit through their shared story of persecution (Kepler for witchcraft; Hindemith by the Nazis in Germany). He was obsessed with the idea that Kepler had discovered music in the organization of the heavens and planets: that in the planetary proportions were the spatial and spiritual aspects of music. Kepler had claimed that there were musical moments in the planets' march around the sun, as if in a "cosmic music box." But all they knew in 1619, when Kepler wrote his treatise, were the planets as far out as they could see, stopping at Saturn; they were not aware yet of the outer planets. This subject came up through Hindemith's class called A History of the Theory of Music, which covered all polyphonic music. Leading a huge group of students, he had us perform music of that early polyphonic time—the fifteenth to the sixteenth century, and in some cases with original instruments, which we got mostly from the Metropolitan Museum of Art in New York. The Met had a great collection of ancient instruments, exotic crumhorns, and all. And several times, those of us who were jazz-inclined said, "My goodness, this cat, Anonymous, is someone that Bird would really dig! And he's playing it on a crumhorn, which predated the saxophone by several hundred years!" I thought this was just fantastic, and I myself was unable to forget about that cosmic music box out there and wondered about it often.

Upon graduating from Yale, I joined Lionel Hampton's band, and traveled and recorded with just about everybody of importance in the jazz field. In the early 1970s, I was invited to come back to Yale and join the faculty at the School of Music where I found myself teaching in the same room where Hindemith had taught his class about Kepler. Kepler had thrown out a challenge to his contemporaries—the musicians and the scientists of his time—with those consonant and dissonant rhythmic moments, and the cosmic march of time where there was music that could be set to sacred texts or perhaps songs. Kepler knew how to find such moments, but he would have had to do so much work to reproduce them, and there was no mechanism in place to do it during his lifetime, or even during Hindemith's lifetime. But by the time I came back in the early 1970s, there were— you could guess what—computers.

So, finally, there was this opportunity to take on Kepler's challenge. I enlisted the help of one of Yale's, and the world's, greatest geologists, the great stratigrapher, John Rodgers. Rodgers was also a great musician, and we used to play Hindemith's chamber music together when we were both residents of Branford College. John was a wonderful mathematician, and when I talked to him about collaborating with me, he suggested that we work in the dining halls at lunch and dinner, where students could gather around and we could attempt to develop a computer program that would take on Kepler's challenge—sketched on napkins and the backs of envelopes. We worked on that together for nearly one year, a feat that was not achievable in Kepler's own time, or even Hindemith's. We sought to give expression to the three laws of planetary motion, to create a Planetarium for the Ear.

Soon, we had everything we needed to develop a computer program; Yale didn't have much computation equipment at that time— hardly any school did—but Princeton happened to sit in the backyard of Bell Labs in New Jersey. A very creative musician there named Milton Babbitt, who knew more about jazz than just about anybody I knew, got some of the executives at Bell Labs to give us some computer time in the off-hours (like between two and five in the morning) for graduate students to conduct our work. And, after a while, we had a realization for the "Planetarium of the Ear" that Kepler had predicted was there. We had some difficulties in the old days, as everyone familiar now with computers might imagine. For instance, if you gave the computer some suspicious data or task to do, it would tell you to "Go to hell!" and spit all of your data out on the floor; and it did just that, several times. But after a while, we had what we needed, and that was the sound of all nine of the planets. The excitement about that realization was so intense worldwide that it actually made the front page of the Tuesday Science Section of the *New York Times* on April 24, 1979.

The next day, my telephone rang in my office in Branford College.

"Is this Professor Ruff?"

I said, "Yeah."

"This is Carl Sagan from Jet Propulsion Lab, and we're about to send out a spacecraft in search of extraterrestrial intelligence, and we saw what you'd accomplished with Kepler's three laws of planetary motion and we'd like to include that in the recording."

And that did happen, and one of the places I first unfurled that on the Yale campus was in Kent Bloomer's class. We came with just the sound of the nine planets in the configuration where they would appear sequentially. But since that time, all of you wonderful taxpayers have helped NASA and other agencies like Hubble send out spacecraft with telescopes, so we now have images of the nine planets along with the sound, and I want to share that with you.[1]

Jesus, that was a hell of a lot of fun.

Note

1. For additional information see Jonathan Scott, *The Vinyl Frontier: The Story of NASA's Interstellar Mixtape* (New York: Bloomsbury, 2019).

1. The Voyager 1 Golden Record is prepared for installation on the spacecraft. Photograph from NASA/JPL-Caltech.

III. STUDIO

REDISCOVERING THE ORNAMENT

Gary Huafan He

Gary Huafan He is an architect and scholar interested in the intellectual and material history of ornament in relation to modernity and modernism in architecture. He holds a doctoral degree in the history and theory of architecture from Yale University.

It is impossible to attempt to give something like an overview or synopsis of the oeuvre of Kent Bloomer through a simple chronological account of his teaching and work, both of which span more than half a century. More than an energetic accumulation of writings, sculptures, and architecture, Bloomer's intensely productive focus on ornament cannot be separated, I argue, from their fundamental theoretical suppositions. Those who know Kent will understand the importance he attributes not only to physical ornaments and their designs, but also to the constant pursuit of ornament as a sensibility and idea. Those who have conversed with him at length on these topics will know that this pursuit is not rooted in any dogmatic or pre-ordained perspective, but rather is an active, changing, and ever-evolving journey which combines a mixture of scholastic, creative, and biographical elements. It must be said from the very beginning that Kent is no traditionalist: though he is never shy to plunge into historical texts or track down the etymological roots of ancient concepts, it is never for want of reinforcing classical or traditional structures or genealogies.

If anything, Kent's educational trajectory was exactly the opposite of traditional: he'd come to architecture at MIT in 1956 through a background in physics, before studying sculpture at Yale with Josef Albers. Kent's account of the Albers school was that of a supreme emphasis on the intersubjectivity of art and its viewer; the artist's greatest task was positioning the artwork in relation to the body of the person looking at it. Here he was met with a definition of sculpture as an autonomous or self-sufficient piece within an "undifferentiated" context, an idea which his training in architecture and its role in the urban fabric could not accept unchallenged. It is perhaps out of this initial resistance that Kent rediscovered the ornament, which, put most simply and directly, is a work that insists on its contextuality. Kent's first sculptures of this period of the late fifties to sixties were cold-forged out of steel, brass, and aluminum which were then assembled with rivets, like medieval armor plating, if only armor grew skyward out of the ground in an expression of its own foliation. In keeping with the pedagogical demands of the Albers school, the naturality concealed in the abstract, twisting forms of the early *Gestalter* were sufficiently "pure" and object-like (figures 1–7), but, in retrospect, were already hinting at the contingent notion of connectivity through the presence of clamps that situate them to a ghosted body. Thus, out of the modernist study of figure-ground, open and closed, stable and unstable forms emerged the shy beginnings of two concepts that would continue to grow in importance in Kent's work: a steeped interest in nature and natural forms on the one hand, and the supplementarity of ornament on the other. The two concepts would find their earliest synthesis in the sculptures "Intersection," "Corner," and "Co-Existence" (figures 8–11) produced in the seventies and eighties. Each of these works introduces a freestanding wall out of which the now more explicitly leaf-shaped plates are cut, bent, and folded, before being allowed to fall, as if from a tree, downward and through the wall again. What is being rehearsed here in sculpture, which at the same time was being translated into full-scale projects, is the ancient dance between the contrapuntal and syntactic points of foliated ornament and the more conventional elements of architectural construction.

It must be said that if Kent's pursuit of ornament involved an intellectual rediscovery of its most enduring properties, it was also driven by a rebelliousness fueled by a pervasive anti-ornament atmosphere at Yale and other institutions of architecture education which persist, in some degree, to this day. He recalls, as an amicable young faculty member interested in learning and teaching the subject, deciding to omit the word "ornament" from his syllabi and pedagogical repertoire, a candid example of how concepts are never simply linguistic devices, but can be charged with often unresolved and contradictory content better left undiscussed. But as a jazz percussionist, someone who practiced daily pitting irresolution and improvisation against the ground of stable rhythm, Kent understood well that blanket antagonisms were never rooted in creative activity, but rather only served ideological purposes. The counterculture to the avant-garde is *not* conservative but rather produces a third critical direction, for the avant-garde is never as progressive as it likes to think itself.

Against this backdrop, Kent took on commissions increasingly architectural in scale. The sculptural facade that he created in 1965 after winning the competition of the new Freehof Hall at the Rodef Shalom Congregation in Pittsburgh (figure 12) displayed a masterful control of wave-form geometry in a concrete field, a physical achievement whose beauty played out primarily in light and shadow. Ornament for Kent was not reserved only for specific building or program types. It was not a mark of prestige or status, but rather found itself equally at home as an aluminum and steel Tree Dome for the Wonderwall at the 1984 Louisiana World's Fair (figures 20–23), that "Stationary Mardi Gras Parade" designed by Charles Moore, a theme repeated as a leafy trellis sprouting from metal members at the Ronald Reagan National Airport, completed in 1997 (figures 13–14). Rather than spaces for the scrutinous connoisseurship of fine art, these ornaments occupied the scenes of the passing and celebration of everyday life. The site of Kent's largest contribution of civic ornament at this period was at the Harold P. Washington Library in Chicago, where he was commissioned in 1990 to design ornament for five iconic owls (figures 17–19) to be set atop the building designed by architect Thomas Beeby, which the critic Paul Goldberger called a "sumptuous, 10-story classical structure with a lavish array of detail that at once recalls the opulent Beaux-Arts architecture of Europe and the powerful, heavy masonry structures of an ascendant Chicago."[1] But, when Kent speaks of the work, he points to its modernity, and how massive owls and acroterion could never have appeared to be resting upon the shimmering structures of a delicate foliated glass pediment at that scale in any previous time. Very few students of architecture today would stop and wonder if the nocturnal raptor that overlooks visitors who approach and enter the library is a reincarnation of the mythological Owl of Minerva, and even fewer would further inquire whether it is meant to directly challenge the eagle, an ornament trope prominent in the nineteenth century as a sigil of French imperialism which might have otherwise stood in its perch.

And yet, such questions—obscure, indirect, hypothetical, and open—have been the subject of my conversations with Kent over the past few years at Yale. Kent took a welcomed interest in my research on the sociality of ornament and its oscillation or sometimes simultaneity between universal symbol, work of art, or social signifier (which Kent calls decoration). We were not always in complete alignment, nor should we be, but we discussed at length on the phenomenon that the slippage between these various roles seemed embedded in the concept of ornament itself. Kent viewed ornament as an essential property of architecture, though not one borne of the "necessity" of any specific function—it was fundamentally expressive of our relationship to nature—in it, around it, against it, as part of it. To which I would respond in challenge, yes, but isn't nature, once reified as form, immediately at the moment of its creation brought inevitably into the realm of the social, into a particular point in space and time which is permeated with its specific political, cultural, and economic conditions? And does this form not accumulate and take on, over time, specifically cultural values and meanings perhaps completely unanticipated or even expressly perpetuated by the sculptor, or his client, or the bureaucratic institutions to which they belong? Do ornaments not sometimes lose their body, and thus their function of ornamenting, to become isolated as separate commodities in the architectural marketplace, or perhaps placed alone as alienated works of art against the "undifferentiated" background of a museum? Kent's response, which I believe to be of great importance and consequence, and bears the clarification of potential misunderstanding, was that yes, all of these things can happen to an ornament and its form, but *ornament itself is not tied to its form in the first place*. Ornament was fundamentally operative, a verb, an act which has its own temporality and historicity regarding the expression of the natural world and our changing knowledge of it, a prime example being Kent's own work at the Yale Chemistry Research Building, in which molecular models are woven into the steel and bronze gate (figure 15). If there is something like an aesthetic ideal for Kent, it would not be ornament *qua* nature, but that of nature *qua* ornament.

There is, therefore, something like an inbuilt metaphoric distance which sets itself in distinct opposition to concepts like biomimesis, the formal or structural imitation of natural forms made so fashionable in recent decades by the advent of digital technologies and computation in architecture. Rather, Kent's work continues to be predicated fundamentally on bringing attention to human connectivity and civic engagement. The 2015 project for Slover Library in Norfolk, Virginia (figure 24) is perhaps his most volumetric and spatial work to date: a 40 x 80 x 40-foot glass enclosure, throughout which is distributed an enormous program of foliated ornament. It sits between an existing Beaux-Arts building and a new seven-story tower and commercial complex, serving as a new "forum" for gatherings, events, and congregation of the neighborhood. Likewise, his most recent work for a new plaza in Alexandria, Virginia (figure 25) is carved out of the mass of a 1.25-million-square-foot mixed-used building structure. The massive space is to be visually unified by a system of ornament, rather than by signage or by a composition of familiar building types. In his words, the realm of living nature *qua* ornament, is choreographed to permeate and pervade human habitation within the dense urban complex. In the same breath—and this is true of Kent as an artist and scholar—his transcendence is immediately and always grounded in community.

In his own essay, which appears later in this volume, Kent invokes the concept of *kosmos* in Isidore of Seville's ancient *Etymologies* to ponder the reflective relationship between natural and man-made objects. If a classical source for architecture has always been the precarity of the human condition *vis a vis* nature, a nature from which inspiration is derived as much as shelter is needed, such a precarity is perhaps now complicated by an increasing consciousness of the inverse situation—the devastating exactitude of humankind's deteriorating relationship with the natural world. It is perhaps easy in our present context of material scarcity to revive the charge of ornament's supplementarity as allegedly "opulent" or "decadent," to the point of criminality towards the environment (I would argue just the opposite), and bring up Kent's point once more of ornament as not necessary but *essential*. It is precisely in this time of crisis that we may benefit most from the innovation and integration of ornament with architecture in environmentally creative ways. In the time of digital fabrication and recyclable raw materials, designers, sculptors, and architects may learn to look at the negative space created *around* ornament as a net gain against otherwise unadorned but solid volumes and surfaces. It may be Kent's reading of *kosmos* as an ontological condition—nature in its ultimate sublimity—which in the final analysis most urgently buttresses our own historical reading of nature as one whose compatibility with our species may be catastrophically limited, by reminding us that it is we who must come to understand and strive to synergize with the rhythms and motions of nature, and that to this end there is much more to be done.

Note

1. Paul Goldberger, "Architecture View; Chicago Unveils a Proud New Temple of Books," *The New York Times*, March 1, 1992.

1. Kent Bloomer, *Brass Sculpture*, 1958.

2. Kent Bloomer, *Brass Sculpture*, 1958.

3. Kent Bloomer, *Little Flat*, brass, 1961.

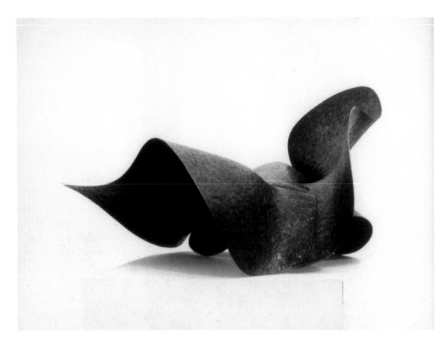

4. Kent Bloomer, *Big Flat*, brass, 1964.

5. Kent Bloomer, *Brass Sculpture*, 1958.

6. Kent Bloomer, *Brass Sculpture*, 1958.

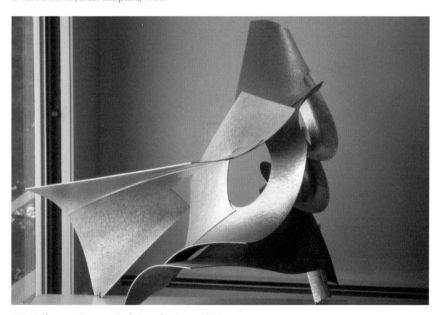

7. Kent Bloomer, *Downey Sculpture*, aluminum, 1984.

8. Kent Bloomer, *Intersection*, aluminum, 1978.

9. Kent Bloomer, *Corner Piece*, aluminum, 1980.

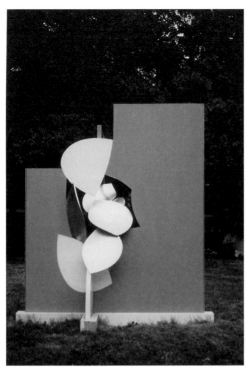

10. Kent Bloomer, *Co-existence*, aluminum and wood, 1981.

11. Kent Bloomer, *Northshore Lobby*, aluminum, 1982.

12. Kent Bloomer, *Rodef Shalom Bas Relief,* concrete, 1965. Photograph by Kent Bloomer.

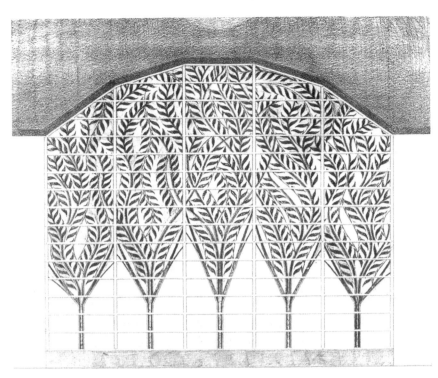

13. Kent Bloomer, *Ronald Reagan Washington National Airport Trellis*, drawing, 1997.

14. Kent Bloomer, *Ronald Reagan Washington National Airport Trellis*, aluminum, 1997.

15. Kent Bloomer, *Chemistry Gate at Yale University*, steel and bronze, 2005. Photograph by David Lamb Photography.

16. Kent Bloomer, *Bartels Staircase*, steel and bronze, 2002. Photograph by David Lamb Photography.

17. Kent Bloomer, *Harold Washington Chicago Library Acroterion*,
aluminum, 1993. Photograph by Kent Bloomer.

18. Kent Bloomer, *Harold Washington Chicago Library Seedpod Acroterion*, aluminum, 1993.
Photograph by Kent Bloomer.

19. Kent Bloomer, *Harold Washington Chicago Library Seedpod* (under construction), aluminum, 1993. Photograph by Kent Bloomer.

20. Kent Bloomer, *Wonderwall Tree Dome Model*, 1982.

21. Kent Bloomer, *Wonderwall Tree Dome*, aluminum, 1984.

22. Kent Bloomer, *Wonderwall Collage*, paper, 1964.

23. Kent Bloomer, *Wonderwall Tree Dome*, Swenson's Ice Cream Parlor, aluminum and steel, 1984.

24. Kent Bloomer, *Slover Memorial Library, Norfolk, VA*, 2015. Photography by Peter Aaron/OTTO.

25. Kent Bloomer, *Carlisle Plaza, Alexandria, VA,* drawing, 2019.

IV. LEGACIES

THE PLACE
OF MURALS

Douglas Cooper

Douglas Cooper is Andrew Mellon Professor of Architecture and an adjunct faculty member with the Carnegie Mellon University School of Architecture.

I've known Kent Bloomer since I was his student in the fall of 1965 at what was then called Carnegie Tech in Pittsburgh. That year—it would be his last in Pittsburgh before leaving for Yale—he taught drawing.

1965 was perhaps the height of what Kent calls the "Modernist Project" in his book *The Nature of Ornament*.[1] But even then, there were strong hints of what his work on ornament would yield: a full-on assault on the sterile neutrality of the stripped-down architecture of the day and its reductionist principles: that all locations shall be equal; that the surfaces shall be only "themselves"; and that, if anything might be expressed, it shall only be structure.

As I read Kent's words, most of all in the last several pages of his book, I recognize a common purpose that my work shares with his, and with the work of ornament more generally: an intention to make places. "By incorporating visions of the world at large and convening with ordinary and profane things, ornament can articulate the complexity and mythology of particular times and places."[2] Though it was impossible to know it at the time, Kent's drawing course would lead me into a career of ornamenting buildings with murals.

Ornament: Seeing a Place and Knowing a Place

> "ornament . . . can intermingle with a particular history and
> with local flora and fauna"

At first, Kent's drawing course was a puzzle. It met only once a week, and it was comprised of a semester-long assignment, which we freshmen all thought was impossible. On this first day, Kent asked us to draw the inside of our studio and everything outside it as well—and all in one drawing. Then he left the room, saying he'd be back in a week to have a look. Insides and outsides? We were all dumbfounded, but I owe my career to this assignment and to this man.

His assignment had a lot to do with his practice as a sculptor. Accustomed to working in three dimensions, he was suspicious of the fundamental illusion of drawing—two dimensions representing three— and he questioned the value of linear perspective because of its limitation to one viewpoint. He somehow wanted to free drawing from the limitation of describing what we might see at any one point in time and use it, instead, to address our experience of our subject over time: to see it, but also to know it.

As we worked, Bloomer showed us images from the period before the Renaissance rediscovery of linear perspective: illuminated manuscripts and the works of Proto-Renaissance painters such as Giotto, Lorenzetti, and Simone Martini. He showed us how these incorporated multiple views (looking upward at ceilings and downward at floors), and he pointed out their insides and outsides. The one I remember most was *The Effects of Good Government in the City and in the Country,* one of a series of three frescos painted by Lorenzetti (c. 1290–1348) in Siena's Palazzo Pubblico. It is centered on the marketplace inside the city, but also includes the fields and hills outside the city walls (figure 1).

Inspired by this fresco, I experienced Pittsburgh's cityscape in a totally new way. The landscape invited me to look up at the undersides of porches, down steps, and left and right with bending roads (figure 2). As I drew the city's steep terrain, I tilted viewing angles, moved vanishing points, rotated coordinates, and lifted entire neighborhoods from below so that I could reveal the layout of their streets and houses (figure 3). Bloomer's assignment seemed to point to a deeper understanding of how we experience the world around us: some fundamental cognitive map arising from pairing both inside and outside— seeing and knowing together. Over the years, these experiences of Pittsburgh's urban landscapes gave rise to my murals, which have proven to resonate with local inhabitants. Because Kent attaches such emphasis to the "local" in his discussion of ornament, I want to explore this connection with the public by focusing on Pittsburgh as a place and my drawings within that context.

With its geologic legacy as an eroded seabed, Pittsburgh has a singular topography of steep plateaus overlooking rivers, and deep hollows following runs and creeks. It's a city with distinct edges: steep drop-offs at the rims of plateaus, and unbuildable slopes and ravines between them (figure 4). Pittsburgh does not sprawl in the way that a Cleveland or a Detroit does.

Pittsburgh's boundaries shape the ways we move through the city. Steep valley walls have left the city with a distinctive set of paths— whether meandering roads (one of the reasons so many get lost in the city) (figure 5) or city steps of legendary length (figure 6). Pittsburgh is also a city of bridges: 466 of them. These serve as thresholds between neighborhoods throughout the city. Whether we are crossing a river or a ravine, they provide clear signals that we have left one district and are en route to another (figure 16).

By drawing the city over the years, I have discovered that its terrain has created two kinds of places: nested and layered. Nested places have an inside within an outside. They tend to focus on the bounded character of slope communities, such as this view of Polish Hill (figure 7). Or they tend to be map-like, as in this view into a backyard (figure 8), or this view of the Turtle Creek Valley (figure 9). These drawings of nested neighborhoods reflect their strong unifiers—whether a railroad line, a streambed, a factory shed, a man working on a car, or a parish church.

Other neighborhoods are experienced as layered places. They are visual journeys from foreground to background that reveal sequences of interior and exterior spaces. The mural I created for Carnegie Mellon University's Cohon Center provides numerous instances. In one part skewed foreground houses create a neighborhood pocket at night at an intersection high up a slope. The pocket overlooks a map-like daytime view over South Oakland below, which, in turn, overlooks a nighttime view of the Jones and Laughlin blast furnaces along the banks of the Monongahela River further below (figure 10).

Such views are not intended to show what we can see. No one could possibly see all of this from any one position. Rather, they are intended to show what we might see and know. They combine multiple points in historical time, time of day, and positions along a path. They are intended to show what we might see at any one point along a path, but at the same time what we might know about other places along the journey. In this, they are more like pilgrimage maps than panoramic overviews.

Ornament: Place and Anonymity

"It (ornament) shields the object or place from the dreadful anonymity of an existence out of place . . ."

Murals can take ordinary or even forgettable spaces and make them special places. They can transform an ordinary reception desk into an extension of the city's landscape (figure 11). They can incorporate even ugly things, such as these grates that became part of a portico in the Lecture Hall at the University of Rome (figure 12). They can enliven an otherwise empty, curving corridor wall with multiple layers of drawings built over photographs, as in this mural I did for the Carnegie

Mellon University building in Qatar with two photographer collabora-
tors, my daughter Sarah, and her partner Nina Gorfer (figure 13).

The corridor outside of Sullivan Auditorium in Carnegie Mellon's
new Tepper Business School would have been indistinguishable from
similar corridors located throughout the building. Now it is home to
the Collaborative Campus mural, which was a joint effort with my
wife Stefani that explores the cooperative work that has long been
a hallmark of Carnegie Mellon University. Out of our preliminary
sketches, an approach emerged that created an alternating rhythm
of fabric collage and charcoal drawing (figure 14). The four vignettes
depict familiar campus settings focused on the community-building
that is at the heart of collaborative work: students, faculty, staff,
and other professionals in arts, technology, and decision sciences
all working together. The four scenes represent different modes
of working together to create knowledge: ranging from the classic
scientific/academic research approach to project-based teamwork.

The mural speaks of the university's history, culture, and aspirations,
and brings its own colorful and lively architecture to a setting that
might otherwise be a lobby in any contemporary office building, any-
where in the world.

Ornament: Place and Story

> ". . . ornament . . . exalts ordinary properties by incorporating
> extraordinary images and individuals' memories within patterns
> that can intermingle with a particular history"

Until 1943, Renzo, a Jew, had survived the war living more or less
openly in Rome. He was careful to maintain his close friendships with
members of the local civil police from before the war. So it happened
that on that day the Gestapo left their headquarters—right next door
to the local police barracks—his friends on the force tipped him off.
So all the while the SS was there at his home looking for him and
ransacking his house somewhere in Esquilino, he was playing cards
with his police friends right next door to the SS (figure 15).

Individual stories such as this are found throughout the mural
at the University of Rome—it's in a building in the Esquilino district,
and the stories are from its residents.

In some murals I've asked people to draw their memories themselves; and then I've puzzled them together into maps of their neighborhoods. This part of the mural at the Heinz History Center in
Pittsburgh shows the city's Hill District (figure 16).

It is assembled out of stories such as this. Anna was living in the
Strip District neighborhood below the Hill when the flood came on
St. Patrick's Day in March 1936. First, she drew her house (figure 17).
When I asked her how high up the water had come, she drew the
water up to her second-story window. Then she drew the events of
the night: first, her downstairs neighbor had torn the front door off its
hinges, put his family on it, and then, using the door as a kind of
kickboard, floated his family to safety. Later, a casket from a nearby
casket factory had floated by. In the early morning, she had looked
down into the backyard and seen terrified cattle from the nearby
stockyards being swept through the backyard by the rushing water.
They were driven against the picket fence where their hooves became
shackled, and they were drowned. By later that day, the water had
reached the second floor and Anna, terrified, ran from window to
window looking for help. In the distance, she saw boats looking for
trapped residents. Prisoners had been let out of jail to man these boats.
Anna could not swim, so she called one over and was rescued.

Some stories are more part of a collective memory of a place. The
King County Courthouse mural series in Seattle addresses the entire
region served by the courthouse: its rural as well as urban areas. My
effort to tie the mural to that larger setting got a substantial boost from
the fact that Seattle was founded after the age of photography had
begun, so I could draw from the rich documentation about the region's
history in the archive of the University of Washington, where I found
images of the city from its earliest days of settlement by immigrants
from the Midwest, when Native American customs and practices were
still part of daily life. Each wall of the courthouse lobby took on an
individual theme. Here are several:

Logging and Mining (figure 18): The upper panel depicts a fictitious
coal town in the early part of the twentieth century. Miners are grimly
entering the hill, where they will spend their next shift underground.
In the right foreground, a woman is scrubbing her husband's head
after his return from the mines. I based the coal-washing facility and
the miner's housing on photographs from the Black Diamond Area.

The lower panel shows logging practices in the Tiger Mountain area over multiple periods of time. Two men stand on what were called "springboards" as they use a crosscut saw to fell a tree. A choker setter, one of the most dangerous jobs in logging, is pulling a line from a steam donkey to the cut logs so they can be dragged to a waiting truck.

Fishing (figure 19): This mural looks out onto what might have been the original state of Elliot Bay. It shows Native Americans fishing on inland streams during salmon runs. Parents are shown in modern dress showing their children how they used weirs to entrap and spear salmon, and the implements they used to prepare fillets for smoking. The man is using a leister. There are cedar plank houses below at the shore of the distant bay. In the distance the ship called the "Exact" is arriving off Alki Point in November 1851 with the Denny party, the first white settlers to the area. Details of the Native American tools and methods shown were based on the work of anthropologist Hilary Stewart.

Related to present-day Native American issues, I spoke with Lois Sweet Dorman, tribal legal counsel for the Snoqualmie Tribe for the disposition of Snoqualmie Falls. Through her, I learned of the multiple meanings people attach to the same place: the Falls (figure 20).

There were (and still are) competing claims over the Falls from three groups: (1) the Snoqualmie Tribe, for whom the site is sacred; (2) Puget Sound Energy, which operates a hydroelectric plant at the Falls; and (3) various businesses operating below the Falls—primarily hop growers, dairy farmers, and recreational boating companies.

The legal issues were and still are complicated, but I can summarize them this way: the promoters of recreational boating, local farmers, and Puget Sound Energy desire a regulated flow of water; to have a reliable and safe water flow for boating and farming downriver; and to maintain power generation for the turbines.

In opposition, the Snoqualmie require a free flow of water over the Falls. As Lois Dorman explained to me, in their creation story the Moon's mother had a dream at the present location of the Falls (before the Falls existed, the flat bottom of the Sky World). Looking up one night in her dream state, she found her future lover in a star above nearby Mount Si. After she gave birth to Moon, her son returned to the site and created the Falls out of a fish weir to give the Snoqualmie people a place of life-sustaining abundance. In their tradition, the Falls are the place of birth and burial of the Snoqualmie (their vertical axis), and the souls of their dead are carried to their creator by the mists that form when the water of the Falls is flowing freely.

I mapped these two parts—the areas above and below the Falls—into a kind of world map, a *mappa mundi* of the Snoqualmie Tribe centered about the Falls. The area above the door presents the Sky World of the Snoqualmie Tribe: Mount Si, where in the creation story the mother of Moon gave birth to him and where the body of Moon now lies; the Falls pouring over the top of the door form a threshold into the world below. In the foreground of the mural at the base of the Falls, the lower world begins. References to the conflict surrounding the Falls—the power plant, cows, and boaters—are set about what becomes an extended view of the Snoqualmie River heading northward towards Puget Sound.

Between these two worlds stands Lois Dorman, who is still the spokeswoman for the tribe concerning the Falls. I was not seeking to resolve the dispute with this composition, only to show that the one unifying element in it was the river itself, and that in the consideration of the river's long-term health might be found its one viable solution.

Spirit and Place

In looking at my own work, I see these three ways that can be seen as part of Kent's legacy: portraying our experience of the city as both what we see and what we know; transforming anonymous space into places; and celebrating our individual and collective stories. The Kent Bloomer I remember from that time in Pittsburgh in 1965 is the one that he has always remained, one who authentically belongs to the place where he is. Though he lived in Pittsburgh for only a few short years, his hammered brass works capture the spirit of the place in ways I find so evident in these pictures that Kent shared with me recently of himself at work in his studio, opposite the Jones and Laughlin Steel Mill (figures 21–22).

Notes

1. Kent Bloomer, *The Nature of Ornament: Rhythm and Metamorphosis in Architecture,* first edition (New York: W.W. Norton, 2000).

2. Ibid., 231.

1. Ambrogio Lorenzetti, *The Effects of Good Government in the City and in the Country*, fresco. Palazzo Pubblico, Siena, Italy: 1337–39. Public Domain.

2. Douglas Cooper, *Game Night*, charcoal on paper on board. Private collection: 2006.

3. Douglas Cooper, *Bigelow Boulevard*, charcoal on paper on board. Private collection: 2015.

4. Douglas Cooper, *St. Joseph's & Immaculate Heart of Mary*, charcoal on paper on board. Collection of the artist: 2018.

5. Douglas Cooper, *Back of Route 30*, charcoal on paper on board. Private collection: 2015.

6. Douglas Cooper, *Steps Down from Mission*, charcoal on paper on board. Westmoreland Museum of American Art, Greensburg, PA: 2006.

7. Douglas Cooper, *Immaculate Heart of Mary*, charcoal on paper on board. Private collection: 2012.

8. Douglas Cooper, *Backyard Auto Repair*, charcoal on paper on board. Private collection: 2011.

9. Douglas Cooper, *Morning Arrivals in Turtle Creek*, charcoal on paper. Private collection: 1999.

10. Douglas Cooper, *Cohon Center Mural (detail)*, charcoal on paper on board. Carnegie Mellon University, Pittsburgh, PA: 1996.

11. Douglas Cooper with Grégoire Picher, *Michael Baker Lobby Mural (before and after)*, charcoal on paper on board. Pittsburgh, PA: 2003.

12. Douglas Cooper with Grégoire Picher and Patty Culley, *University of Rome (southeast corner before and after)*, charcoal on paper on board. Rome, Italy: 2005.

13. Douglas Cooper with Sarah Cooper and Nina Gorfer, *Carnegie Mellon at Qatar Mural*, charcoal and photo montage on board. Doha, Qatar: 2009.

14. Douglas Cooper and Stefani Danes, *Carnegie Mellon University Tepper School of Business Mural*, charcoal and fabric on board. Carnegie Mellon University, Pittsburgh: 2019.

15. Douglas Cooper, *Renzo's Story*. Mural in Ex Caserma Sani, Universitá Roma Tre, Rome, Italy: 2005.

16. Douglas Cooper, *Hill District Map*. Senator John Heinz History Center, Pittsburgh, PA: 1992.

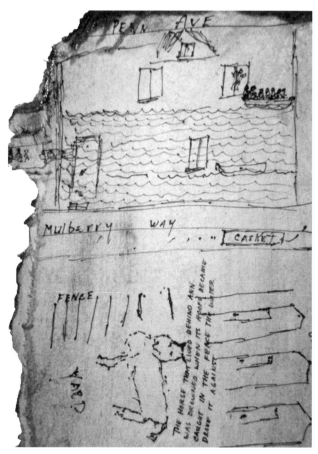

17. Douglas Cooper, *Anna's Story*. Senator John Heinz History Center mural,
Pittsburgh, PA: 1992

18. Douglas Cooper with Grégoire Picher and Patty Culley, *Logging and Mining*, charcoal on paper on board. King County Courthouse, Seattle, WA: 2005.

19. Douglas Cooper with Grégoire Picher and Patty Culley, *Fishing*, charcoal on paper on board. King County Courthouse, Seattle, WA: 2005.

20. Douglas Cooper with Grégoire Picher and Patty Culley, *Snoqualmie Falls*, charcoal on paper on board. King County Courthouse, Seattle, WA: 2005.

21. Kent Bloomer, *Brass Sculpture*, 1968.

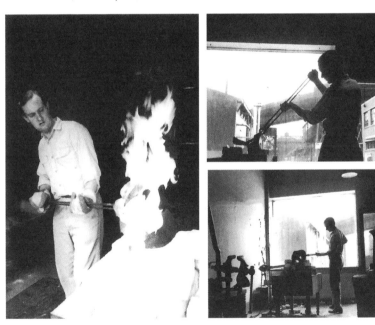

22. Kent Bloomer in his studio, c. 1965.

BEAUTY AND THE ART OF ROUGHNESS

Emer O'Daly

Emer O'Daly is an Ireland-based architect engaged in the theory of fractals. She trained as an architect at University College Dublin and Yale University.

Beauty is a word that has fallen out of favor. However, I believe that it is a subject worth talking about. So, what do we mean when we talk about beauty? Although it is not easily defined, I think most can agree that there is beauty to be found in nature—in trees and foliage, landscapes, mountains, and water. As architects, we are accustomed to thinking about the formal language of man-made structures. So what is the formal language of nature? When we look at the forms of nature, what we see is a sort of roughness; a seemingly chaotic array of shapes and meandering lines. These are not forms that we can easily describe with the classical geometry of spheres, cubes, and cones.

> "Clouds are not spheres, mountains are not cones, coastlines are not circles, and bark is not smooth, nor does lightning travel in a straight line."

So said mathematician Benoit Mandelbrot, who in 1976 revolutionized our understanding of the mathematics and the patterns underlying the natural world. He had discovered a form of order within the seemingly chaotic natural world, and he called this ordering system fractal geometry.

Fractal geometry is a mathematics that comes the closest to finding a way of describing and measuring natural forms. Natural phenomena known to have fractal features include coastlines, mountain ranges, ocean waves, snowflakes, trees, lightning, algae, crystals, and earthquakes. And within ourselves, our brains, our DNA, and our heart rates have fractal attributes. Fractal geometry goes to the very essence of who we are.

There are two salient properties of fractal geometry:

1) Its ability to measure roughness. This property can be illustrated with the coastline paradox. This paradox speaks to the fact that a coastline has an indeterminate length because its measured length depends on the scale of measurement. Empirical evidence shows that the smaller the increment of measurement, the longer the measured length becomes. If one were to measure a coastline at the scale of a kilometre, one would get a shorter result than if the same stretch were measured with centimeters. Laying the centimeter ruler along a

more meandering route results in a longer measurement for
the coastline, when compared to the kilometer ruler. This is
essentially a property of a fractal structure.

2) The second property of fractals is that of self-similarity.
Fractals exhibit symmetries across scales. What this means
is that an object in its entirety is similar to parts of itself.
Examples of this would be branching trees, turbulence in
water, plants, coastlines, and mountain ranges.

Although the word fractal is relatively new, ideas of self-
similarity and roughness are very old. Examples of artists and
architects using these ideas recur throughout history and among
most cultures. For instance, Leonardo da Vinci drew swirls at
various scales in his Turbulence series to mimic the movement
of water; Katsushika Hokusai used wave forms at a number of
scales to illustrate a seascape; Jackson Pollock is recognized as
an artist who created painting with underlying fractal structures.
In fact, neuroscientists have shown that Pollock's paintings induce the same stress reduction in observers as fractals in nature.
     There are further examples of fractal geometry arising in man-
made objects. An eighteenth-century sketch of a Rococo table
(figure 1) may be juxtaposed with a portion of the Mandelbrot set
(figure 2). Using the box-counting method, the fractal dimension
of the table interior is calculated as 1.23. This result indicates that
the dimension as measured is larger than the dimension of a
line. So, roughness becomes a measurable property in all things.
Appropriately, Mandelbrot refers to the forms that emerge in the
Mandelbrot Set as "extraordinary baroque decorations."
     In *The Analysis of Beauty* (figure 3), eighteenth-century British
art theorist William Hogarth explores the rules of composition of
form in the design of a candlestick. Hogarth states that "the art
of composing well is no more than the art of varying well." He
goes on to explain this process of achieving better form:

> 1) "let every distance or length of divisions differ from the length
> of the socket, as also vary in their distances from each other"

2) "let any two points, signifying distance, be plac'd farthest from any other two points, observing always that there should be one distance or part larger than all the rest; and you will readily see that variety could not be so complete without it."[1]

He then warns against subdividing further because "it will want distinctness of form on a near view, and lose the effect of variety at a distance." In Hogarth's description, he advocates for the combination of a variety of lengths of "crinkle" in order to produce a well-composed form. He also advises scale invariance, that is, self-similarity. He protests against the use of similar lengths, but instead indicates that various lengths at various scales produce a more pleasing effect. Hogarth is effectively proposing that self-similarity at various scales, which introduces contrast in length or size in an overall form, is aesthetically pleasing.

The American architect Louis Sullivan wrote about how the form of the ornament must emerge from the character of the architectural whole. He compares the design of an ornamental system to the growth patterns at different scales in nature: "a certain kind of ornament should appear on a certain kind of structure, just as a certain kind of leaf must appear on a certain kind of tree. An elm leaf would not 'look well' on a pine-tree—a pine-needle seems more 'in keeping.'" Here again is an architect advocating for self-similarity.[2]

Sullivan often wrote about the process of "awakening" an architectural form. He would begin with a Euclidean shape, often a pentagon or a circle, and through various symmetry operations and elaborations of the form he would transform it into ornament that "almost literally had life." This method of developing an ornament may be seen in Sullivan's *A System of Architectural Ornament*, in a process he calls the "awakening of the pentagon." He succeeds in converting rigid geometries into lifelike forms (figure 4).

By comparing Louis Sullivan's sketches to several iterations of the Koch fractal, you can see a similar transformation from purely Euclidean shapes through a series of operations to create a more complex, more life-like form. It could be said that Sullivan had discovered a way of introducing a fractal dimension to his forms.

Ornament as Fractal Boundary

In nature, fractals appear at the boundaries of natural forms. In architecture, ornament appears at the boundaries of architectural forms. This can be illustrated by comparing the outline of the National Galerie in Berlin with the Palais Garnier in Paris (figure 5). Clearly, from a distance, the Palais Garnier has a more meandering, rougher outline. The Mies van der Rohe building, in comparison, is much simpler. But, on closer examination, there is a roughness to Mies's details. I think if you took out that little bit of roughness, you would lose a lot of the magic of Mies.

Rough outlines and boundaries do not only appear in Western architecture, but also in most cultures around the world. Traditional Chinese, Indonesian, South American, Mughal, and Indian cultures enriched their buildings with repeating forms and patterns at various scales, often over the entirety of the building. In the temple complex at Angkor Wat, the overall conical shape of the temple reappears at the scale of ornament, covering the surface with these repeating volumetric forms. The use of fractal forms in the ornament and surfaces of architecture seems to be common to all human cultures.

Metamorphosis

In nature, fractals assist in the metamorphosis from one state to another. For instance, the exterior surface of a cloud may be described as the transition zone between air moisture and its surroundings. The metamorphosis between one state and the next is achieved with a fractal boundary—the cloud itself.

In architecture, it is the ornament or detail that allows forms to metamorphose from one into the next. One of the primary functions of ornament is to mediate between different surfaces, volumes, materials, and spaces. It is common for ornament to fill the interstitial spaces in architecture—the gaps, the transition zones between elements, the height disparities between parts—and to bind an entire composition of architectural forms together. Throughout the history of architecture, ornament has often articulated how floor meets wall and wall meets ceiling; how roof meets sky.

In the words of Kent Bloomer, "The principle strategy required to achieve an image of combination in ornament is to present a spectacle of transformation. In that spectacle, it may appear that one thing is turning into another and vice versa." Henri Focillon, in *The Life of Forms in Art*, also identifies ornament as "the chosen home of metamorphoses."[3]

A study of the construction of the Palais Garnier in Paris illustrates this process of metamorphosis. In the photograph taken during the construction of the opera house (figure 6), the utilitarian elements of the building can be seen taking shape, but each element is blocked out in simple Euclidean forms. The bare forms of the columns, capitals, and entablatures are eventually encrusted with ornament of all kinds. The ornament eases the way from one form to the next, and it does this by creating a fuzziness, a crinkle of boundary, and a cragginess to the edges of architecture.

Ornament lends the forms of those buildings a fractal dimension. Most forms in nature have a fractal edge, and therefore supplying such an edge to an object gives it a more natural appearance. The desire for ornament is essentially the desire to make something appear more natural, and therefore more beautiful.

Benoit Mandelbrot described fractal shapes as "grainy, hydralike, inbetween, pimply, pocky, ramified, seaweedy, strange, tangled, tortuous, wiggly, wispy, wrinkled."[4]

Similarly, in architecture, these characteristics can also be used to describe the undulating surfaces and edges of much ornamented architecture (figure 7). When we see crinkled profiles and staggered edges in man-made forms, we are seeing the influence of fractal geometry in our designs. Additionally, this fractal aspect to buildings can only become complete at the scale of ornament. When architects say that ornament "imports" or "super-adds" a new element into a building, along with the cultural significance and symbolic meaning it imbues, it also brings with it, quite literally, a new dimension. Ornamentation gives the edges of the form a fractal dimension. In this way, the fractal dimension, and the degree of ornamentation, become a measurable properties of an object or space. And the art of creating ornament is essentially the art of creating roughness in architecture.

Most architects today rely on a formal vocabulary that is heavily in favor of simplicity at both the large and small scale, resulting in smooth, featureless surfaces. This is the legacy of Modernism in architecture, and unfortunately has created a lot of the blandness and uniformity that we see around us. Streets upon streets of smooth, homogenously surfaced buildings are not appealing in the same way that a medieval city is. Although Modernism can create beautiful objects, it has failed in creating beautiful urban fabric. When we stripped ornament from our buildings, we also eliminated much of the visual complexity and meaning that these forms lent our architecture. As a result, buildings lost much of their uniqueness, character, and color. The homogeneity of modern cities speaks to this reduction in complexity and, in our profession, a loss of the art of roughness.

Digital Craft

The question of beauty in architecture is not solely about aesthetics. Our surroundings affect our well-being at a fundamental level and they have the power to induce joy or despair in us. Grey housing estates, ugly office blocks, lightless hospital rooms, all do damage is ways that we are only beginning to understand. As architects, this is our domain. We are the only ones on the design team who can advocate for beauty.

Fractal geometry tells us that natural landscapes and scenery are beautiful because of the ways in which they are complex. This complexity manifests in rough, meandering surfaces and edge conditions. Beautiful buildings also require complexity at the small scale. There is no way around some form of roughness and therefore, some form of ornament.

Digital fabrication represents a new way of making things that is neither mass manufacturing nor handcraft—it exists somewhere in-between. As our construction practices evolve, the way we build will make uniqueness and complexity ever more feasible again. New ways of making suggest a way forward that is more patterned, colorful and ornamental than anything we have seen in the last one hundred years of architecture.

It is time for architects to turn their minds to beauty again, and rediscover the art of roughness.

Notes

1. William Hogarth, *The Analysis of Beauty. Written with a View of the Fluctuating Ideas of Taste* (Leicester-Fields: 1753), 81.

2. Louis H. Sullivan, "Ornament in Architecture," in *Kindergarten Chats and Other Writings* (New York: Dover, 1979), 189.

3. Kent Bloomer, *The Nature of Ornament: Rhythm and Metamorphosis in Architecture*, first edition (New York: W.W. Norton, 2000), 27.

4. Michael Frame, *Benoit Mandelbrot: a Life in Many Dimensions* (World Scientific Publishing, 2015), 389.

1. Georg Hirt, *Rococo Drawing*, from Das Deutsche Zimmer der Gothik und Renaissance des Barock-, Rococo- und Zopfstils. München & Leipzig: 1886.

2. *Mandelbrot Set*, courtesy Professor David Eck, Department of Mathematics and Computer Science, Hobart and William Smith Colleges.

3. William Hogarth, *The Analysis of Beauty. Written with a View of the Fluctuating Ideas of Taste*, plate 1. Leicester-Fields: 1753.

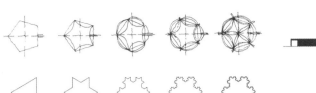 

4. Comparative Diagram of Sullivan, Awakening the Pentagon, drawing by Emer O'Daly.

5. Comparative Diagram of Mies and Garnier, drawing by Emer O'Daly.

6. *Construction of the Grand Staircase of the Palais Garnier (1861–75), Paris, France.* Photograph courtesy of De Agostini Picture Library.

7. *St. Mark's Basilica*, Venice, Italy. Photograph by the author.

8. Emer O'Daly with Love & Robots, *Bowties Horizontal and Vertical.*

Windswept Pendant
€265

PERSONALISE

Bermuda Triangle
10.9 kmph S

PAUSE

Choose Material (Rose Gold Plated)

Made to order: 2-3 weeks to dispatch.

ADD TO CART

SHARE

DETAILS

9. Emer O'Daly with Love & Robots, *Desktop Cloth.*

10, 11. Emer O'Daly with Love & Robots, *Plumage Cape*, 3D-printed.

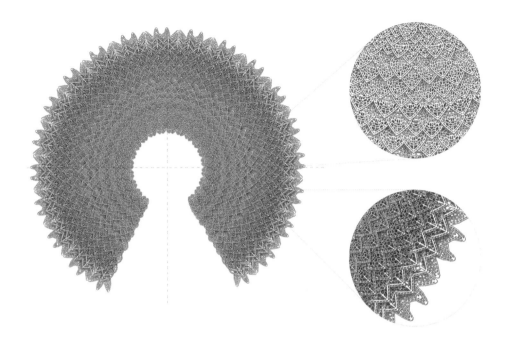

12. Emer O'Daly with Love & Robots, *Plumage Cape Detail*, 3D-printed.

13, 14. Emer O'Daly with Love & Robots, *Plumage Cape Substructure*, 3D-printed.

ATTENTION AND AESTHETICS OF THE BACKGROUND

Michael Young

Michael Young is an architect and educator practicing in New York City, where he is an assistant professor at the Cooper Union. He is a founding partner of the architectural design studio Young & Ayata.

Ornament attracts; Decoration diffuses.

Often confused as equivalent, but performing very different roles, ornament and decoration have occupied a marginal position in architectural discourse over the past century. It is common to encounter discussions on materiality, tectonics, signification, color, pattern, etc., but with much less frequency, ornament and decoration. By putting these two terms in the context of manners of attention, the hope is to reengage their fundamental importance for architectural aesthetics.

Before moving into a more thorough discussion of attention, it is necessary to describe a few key differences between how ornament and decoration operate. Decoration relates to cultural conventions of decorum. The aesthetic impact of decoration can be described as evoking specific moods, atmospheres, or character. These are often allusions and illusions intimately tied to how people understand what constitutes an allowable form of behavior in space. Through this, decoration is always political, operating in the background, just below consciousness, as a diffusion of attention.

Ornament is foregrounded. It wants to be seen, studied, interpreted. It is traditionally a figure, a motif, an identifiable object that has something to communicate. In architecture, ornament often occurs at key moments in the building's articulation. A well-known example is the column capital, which in Post-Renaissance architecture became identified through the classification of "the orders." A capital draws attention to the crucial juncture between column and beam, between vertical and horizontal; it is the knot that binds, the object that focuses, and the symbol that communicates. Ornament animates the static stability of architecture, often through references to the dynamics of the natural world.[1]

One aspect of ornament and decoration that leads to a confusion between the terms is that the repetition of ornament can create a decorative background.[2] Often, the two terms operate together in a rhythmic alternation. In this light, it is more accurate to understand the classical orders as decorum; as decoration. The column capital is an ornamental motif standing as an identifiable symbol for the classification, but *the order* is the entire system of repeated ornaments, proportional control, intercolumniation, sculptural friezes, and coded

articulations, all participant in ordering the affects deemed appropriate
by convention for the purpose of a specific architecture.

> "One distinction between the two can be briefly summarized by
> proposing that decoration is the pleasurable arrangement of elements
> that articulate societal values, order, and beauty, while ornament is
> constituted by motifs that are repetitively distributed about structural
> and decorative elements to evoke natural cycles, efflorescence, and
> transformation. Thus, while decoration visualizes a human dreamscape
> by assembling scenic furnishings to mark and enhance the rituals of
> domestic and civic space, ornament alludes to a rhythmized presence
> of nature wandering through the basic physical framework of design.
> Their visual contents perform differently as they mimic formations
> innate to distinct worlds of the imagination."[3]

In these definitions put forward by Kent Bloomer, decoration is
tied to cultural and social values, while ornament is related to natural
forces at a deeper level, one that Bloomer would characterize as
"cosmic." Also implied is the concept of appropriateness. Decoration
develops a compositional orderliness for producing "good behavior."
Ornament in Bloomer's distinction is more unruly, "mercurial," and
involved in "transferential antics."[4] This aspect is expanded in the
quote above as "a rhythmized presence of nature wandering through
the basic physical framework of design."[5] The question of rhythm is
not only important for the symbolic or iconic references of motifs, it
is also present in the dynamic fluctuation established between close
and diffused attention.

Although not explicitly stated by Bloomer, for decoration to exert
its societal influence it operates in the background of our environments. Decoration strives to create an "all-over" effect, it often
conceals joints, removes seams, and produces continuities across
material difference. Think of the two most typical decorative applica-
tions; paint and wallpaper. These mask the construction that lies
beneath to create an alternate aesthetic character. The Villa Savoye
is a concrete slab and column building with masonry block walls, but
its aesthetic attitude of dematerialized abstract levitation is enabled
through its decoration of white, peach, and forest green paint. To
extend this point further, the later work of Le Corbusier articulates

concrete surfaces as board-formed "béton-brut." This aesthetic affect, stylistically labeled Brutalism, is often argued as a true expression of material and construction "as found."[6] There is an ethical imperative in this argument as the basis for the aesthetic, but I would argue that after roughly a century of board-formed concrete buildings we have come to understand that the best examples are much more complex than a simple expression of material and construction. The traces of formwork can create different moods and atmospheres by diffusing attention across surfaces, as decoration. The affects can be refined, rough, soft, technical, elegant, or raw, depending on the attitude of the aesthetic.

If the claim of the last paragraph is followed to its possible ends, one may understandably ask, "Is there any undecorated architecture?" The easy answer is no. All architecture articulates its surfaces, which at the most fundamental level is a kind of decoration. But this is a mundane point. Decoration is concerned with how the articulation of a surface produces an aesthetics of the background, a creation of environments with specific affects. Many architects might protest the use of the word decoration to catch all these desires. I believe this sentiment reflects a historical bias against related disciplines such as interior decoration, product and furniture design. In its most extreme form, found in the late 19th century and early twentieth century, the denigration of the terms ornament and decoration reflected a cultural bias that harbored deeply problematic assertions.[7] The belief that "un-decorated" architecture is permanent, necessary, refined, and honest, while "decorated" architecture is ephemeral, superfluous, kitsch, and deceitful is still latent in many contemporary architectural arguments.

Decoration is fundamentally a political act. It empowers or suppresses possible engagements, engenders social scenarios, and is intimately tied to capital as an expression of wealth, power, and social aspirations. These can be oppressive conditions, but it also means that decoration is the battlefield upon which alternate possible expressions find their voice, where resistance can be staged, where the background of how reality looks, feels, and behaves can be challenged to be other than assumed.

If decoration is necessarily found in all architectural expressions, what does this imply for the other term? To quote Bloomer again, "Ornament is an intensely visual phenomenon requiring patience and attention."[8] In other words, ornament focuses and intensifies attention on a specific architectural moment, its meaning dependent on the context being ornamented. Decoration is independent from the surfaces that it is applied to, it can be detached and applied elsewhere, even in its removal, with the surfaces left behind taking on aspects of decoration (decay, ruination, patina, etc.); it is impossible to build an undecorated architecture. This is not the case with ornament. You can remove a capital and the column will still meet the beam. Furthermore, the "removed" capital loses its ornamental signification once disengaged from its specific physical location; it cannot be applied freely elsewhere and still perform its intended effect. This aspect is key. Ornament attempts to communicate, to signify. For this to function, ornament is bound with the context in which it is situated. The column capital is one example, but we can extend this to the frames of doors and windows, cornice lines, the central axis of a facade, the corners of a building, and the base or how an architecture meets the ground. All these locations are different, and the meaning of ornament is transformed from one situation to another. It is thus intimately bound with the object that is ornamented. The object can survive without it, which at one level may appear to make it less necessary than decoration, but in the best examples, ornament intensifies attention, becoming a central concern in the aesthetic experience of architecture.

To link ornament and decoration to the issue of attention is not a new concept. If we consider the École des Beaux-Arts rendering techniques of *mosaïque* (the graphic description of surface in an architectural drawing): we find surfaces articulated to attract attention towards primary spaces and diffuse attention from less important ones. Although referred to as a "rendering technique," this should not be mistaken as having a minor role. The articulation of surfaces through representational imaging was fundamental to understanding and evaluating a design within the École des Beaux-Arts. It transformed the abstraction of the geometric parti towards the mood and character that the building was to evoke. Variation in the imaging of the *mosaïque* allowed issues such as circulation to be clarified, programmatic differences to be understood, style to become perceived, and decorum to be judged. Possessing the appropriate decorum was crucial for the success of a design, whether it was eventually built or not. *Mosaïque* was part of a systematic codification of representation structuring the interpretation of a design through the rendered image: a speculative simulation of effects to be evaluated in relation to experience, sensation, *and* convention.

Architecture and Image, Ornament and Decoration, Close and Diffused Attention; these pairings are intimately tied with any aesthetic agenda for architecture. British High-Tech architecture attracts attention around the fetishized mechanical joint and diffuses it across the image of a smooth field of technological glazing. Strands of American Postmodernism attract attention towards strong referential figural motifs while diffusing the support surfaces into thin decorative fields. Swiss Minimalism sublimates Brutalist expression into precise refined decorations, allowing attention to focus on a single, pure entry void, or a slight twist in a copper cladding. Dutch Neo-modernism developed an architecture of color, graphics, and patterns that turn whole pieces of the building into ornamental attractors when placed in collage-like juxtaposition to banal off-the-shelf assemblies. The list could continue, but what I would like to emphasize is that ornament and decoration are intimately tied to issues of attention and the conceptual/aesthetic agendas of the architecture. The difference between these more recent examples and the historical models of the past lies in the cultural communication through representation. We no longer adhere to the same symbolic motifs that require the classical species of close reading. This is another reason why the two terms we have been dealing with have fallen out of fashion over the past century. Architectural discourse shifted away from the academic vocabulary of Beaux-Arts classicism in order to express a more pragmatic relation between form, material, and technology. The problem with this, as noted above, is that the terms themselves became denigrated, as if they were the problem, severing a rich lineage and leaving the discipline to argue its articulations based on issues outside of aesthetics, primarily morally driven beliefs such as "truth-to-function," "truth-to-material," or "truth-to-construction." I have a distrust of all "truth-to- . . . " statements. They are a way of avoiding the responsibility for the aesthetics of an architecture by hiding behind an apparent ethical honesty. They suppose that there is a deeper connection to reality available through the exposure of material, function, and assembly. They also suppose that any covering, that is, any ornament of decoration, is dishonest and suspicious. However, when an expression of "material, function, and assembly" is deemed successful, it is not because of any "truth-to" ethic, it is because the architecture has developed an aesthetic argument regarding these issues; it is because it has engaged the possibilities of ornament, and decoration.

Distraction

I've described the play between ornament and decoration to be one of close and diffused attention. Another term to address is distraction. As Joshua Cohen and many other critics have illuminated, distraction is part of human culture throughout its development, typically tied to the disruptive acceleration of media technologies.[9] This is a problem that we all share today within the "attention economy" of online interactions. In this, there are numerous concerns for how media is altering our sensorial attention towards our environment, monetizing our gaze, and potentially numbing our ability to discern significant details regarding the appearance of reality. These issues have been raised with each new technological mediation, from social media, to video games, to television, to cinema, to radio—to print culture. Each was considered to threaten our attention to reality.

Distraction can also be described as a mode of attention, one that is not necessarily negative. Continuous, sustained attention is not always feasible, nor necessarily desirable. Distraction allows mental operations to "refresh," it is found in various forms of reverie and creative states of consciousness where the mind wanders in non-linear fashion. To quote Marina van Zuylen from her book *The Plentitude of Distraction*:

> Focus is useless without distraction, and distraction, without motivation and a pinch of single-mindedness, dwindles into listless lethargy. Consider with the philosopher Jacques Ranciere this to-and-fro, the openness that emerges when "words and discourses freely circulate, without a master, and divert bodies from their destinations" engaging them in movements, in the neighborhood of certain words: people, liberty, equality, etc. This free-floating world of words and ideas is not distracting in the way our devices are; yes, it engages us indeed in

multiple directions, each one requiring reflectivity, forcing us to find meaning without instant gratification. The key to this positive distraction lies precisely in the delay, a delay that energizes and creates the free circulation of ideas and affects.[10]

Both ornament and decoration can create states of distraction. The problematic aspects occur when everything is constantly a distraction, when the rhythm between close and diffused attention is lost. This leads to the inability to pay attention to anything, an issue that exists today without doubt, but also occurred at other junctures in cultural history. The abrupt fragmentation of montage in art and cinema was an effort to cut through the noise produced by the overwhelming distraction of modern industrialization.[11] These techniques sought to shock attention through the de-contextualization and re-contextualization of fragments from the everyday. One way to understand the ban on ornament in Modernism was as an attempt to focus attention directly on the objects of modern life. Modern architecture became an abstract, dematerialized rupture inserted collage-like into the maelstrom of the environment. This technique of fragmentation had an impact on attention during the early twentieth century, but within our contemporary mediated world it no longer provides the shock. We exist in a world of de-contextualized fragments, a brew of fact and fiction presented on an even playing field, attention distracted into a hum of constantly churning imagery.

The most common response to our contemporary image culture is fear. This is followed either by a sincere desire to return to "the real," or an irony tinged with cynicism that views the condition with an indifferent shrug. I would argue that our engagement with reality is always initially through aesthetics. The world has always been mediated through culture, architecture among our first interventions. Ornament and decoration are crucial components in how architecture has articulated the tensions between reality and its representation, and through this, how architecture mediates attention within the environment.

The alternation, the rhythm between diffused and close attention, describes an entanglement with the world. It also suggests an alternate way to discuss ornament and decoration without reliance on the analysis of traditional ornamental motifs or an exposé of decorative tropes. What is established in this flux of attention is a relation between aesthetic experience and critical interpretation. Instead of sincerity or irony as our only available responses to contemporary mediation, I would suggest a return to the questions of ornament and decoration as matters of attention.

To explicate these ideas further, I will describe four projects from my practice, Young & Ayata. These projects span from an art object to a functional vessel, an architectural detail to a building.

Exquisite Corpse Cones for Harmen Brethouwer, 2015–18 (figures 1–2): Over the past thirty years the Dutch artist Harmen Brethouwer has developed a series of two objects. One: square panels that hang on the wall; the other: cones that sit on the floor or a pedestal. The square panels are stand-ins for the history of painting. The cones, for the history of sculpture. The forms never change. What is different with each manifestation is the ornament and decoration of the objects. Brethouwer is working his way through the collective human cultural history of ornamental motifs and scenarios tied to these articulations.

Over the course of the past four years, Young & Ayata have developed five cones with Brethouwer. Our take on the project has been to extract motifs from Owen Jones's *Grammar of Ornament.*[12] There are twenty divisions in Jones's treatise. Each of our five cones has four ornamental friezes, thus exhausting the classifications as put forward in the middle of the nineteenth century. The cones are divided into four friezes. Each frieze is developed independently as an improvised decoration using elements extracted from specific plates. These are then combined in a manner similar to the Surrealist parlor game of the Exquisite Corpse. Our concerns were to have the patterns sharply juxtaposed at the rupture of the seams, yet have textural, color, and material qualities drift through the seams. The desire was to create a cone with an aesthetic affect as a diffused totality at the level of decorative, yet have specific moments of ornamental attraction differentiated in each frieze.

Base Flowers, 2015 (figures 3–4): The Base Flowers project explored the tensions between ornament and decoration in an alternate manner. Young & Ayata ostensibly designed a flower vase that could tumble into multiple positions. Each position would have a different character for posing the flower arrangements. The vases themselves were fabricated as a multi-material 3-D print of translucent plastic and an opaque black, involuted coral pattern. These vases thus became what the viewer focused on. While attention was distracted towards the vase, we also designed and fabricated 3-D printed flowers that were hybrids of biological, geological, and technological aesthetics. These are the true ornaments of the project, yet they initially hide within the "real" flowers that share their space. Once the observer realizes that there are artificial flowers as well, a rhythm of attention is established between the flowers and the vase. This rhythm pulls and pushes attention, fluxing between ornament and decoration.

Wall Reveal, 2016 (figures 5–6): The Wall Reveal project was a full-scale fabrication for the SCI-Arc gallery exhibition titled *Close-up,* which explored the contemporary architectural detail post-digital fabrication. Young & Ayata developed a series of details that transformed the typical Fry-Reglet wall reveal. We built four interior corners of standard dimensional lumber, Simpson joist hangers, and half-inch Gypsum board. Into these corners, we jacked four different 3-D printed reveal details of our design. Each detail disturbed the meeting of three planes at the wall-to-ceiling juncture. What a typical wall reveal does (outside of providing an edge to finish the wall and the removal of traditional trim pieces that would ornament the joint) is it turns the wall into an abstract floating entity. It is a form of decoration that adjusts the overall aesthetics of the background of a room. Our details attempted to turn the interior corner into an ornament by focusing attention on the corner itself. But there was one detail of the four that subtly twisted along the edge, creating a sense that the walls were off alignment, slipping past each other. We likened this detail to an estrangement of the background, a disturbed decoration. It functioned in a similar manner to the typical Fry-Reglet detail, but through a slight adjustment it produced a shift in attention towards the background of the interior environment, making the walls themselves look weird.

DL-1310 Apartment Building, 2015–19 (figures 7–9): DL-1310 is a nine-unit apartment building in Mexico City designed by Young & Ayata in collaboration with Michan Architecture. The building is typical in many regards, including the unit plan layouts and the construction system of reinforced concrete bearing walls. We made an argument to the developer that, by pulling the building back from the property lines, we could add an extra floor. This made economic sense, and opened the opportunity to have windows along all four sides. The problem that emerged was that, when future buildings are built on the adjoining sites, the side windows would look directly at blank walls. What we developed to address this issue were a pair of window typologies that rotate into the building's interior to allow oblique views out from every space. This rotation created ruled surfaces along the window heads and sills, transforming the entire facade into a play between ornament and decoration. The board form decoration was kept vertical at the walls and horizontal along the slabs/heads/sills. This shift in articulation created an undulating transformation of the floor slabs as they appeared to thicken and thin with the window rotation. At the same time, the bearing walls were transformed into razor-thin edges along the exterior edge of the window frame. The frame turns into a figurative motif, an ornament, focusing attention along the facade in a dimpled staccato rhythm.

Fluctuations of Attention

These four projects could be comfortably explained through materiality, tectonics, image, signification, color, pattern, etc., yet it seems crucial to me that the terms decoration and ornament be brought to the forefront of the argument. This is primarily because decoration and ornament are fundamentally and unavoidably aesthetic questions. Materiality and tectonics can hide behind an ethics of honestly revealing construction. Image and signification can disappear into the internal discourse of historical reference policed by institutions and academies. Color and pattern can be dismissed as mere stylistic taste. But if all these issues are subsumed under ornament and decoration, and all of them are deemed equally important for the ways in which the built environment alters attention, then we cannot relegate aesthetics to a secondary or subsidiary position. The return of these terms as a central responsibility of architecture refuses to let the discipline be reduced to a professional service of pragmatic problem solving. Architecture is responsible for the aesthetics of the background of reality. This is its cultural legacy. This is its political agency. This is its environmental respect.

These are bold claims, I admit, and it can be said that attention is much more than just an aesthetic concern. Attention is a cognitive issue regarding how humans engage their surroundings. It is a social concern when determining how groups of people are represented in communities. It is clearly an economic issue concerning how and where capital is spent in efforts to channel consumption. And there is an ecological aspect in directing attention towards the detrimental effects that human actions have on environmental processes. All of these are massive issues that seem much more important than aesthetics, ornament, and decoration. But I would follow these comments with a question. In what ways does architecture initially participate in the cognitive, social, economic, or ecological concerns of our world? The response to this seems to continually cycle back to how architecture diffuses and attracts attention. And this fluctuation is aesthetic.

Notes

1. Spyros Papapetros, *On the Animation of the Inorganic* (Chicago: University of Chicago Press, 2012), 131–134.

2. Kent Bloomer, "A Critical Distinction Between Decoration and Ornament," from *306090*, Volume 10: Decoration (New York: 306090 Inc., 2006), 49.

3. Ibid., 49.

4. Ibid., 56.

5. Ibid., 49.

6. Reyner Banham, "The New Brutalism," 1955, republished in *A Critic Writes: Selected Essays by Reyner Banham* (Berkeley: University of California Press, 1996), 11.

7. Juan Jose Lahuerta, *On Loos, Ornament and Crime* (Barcelona: TENOV, 2015) 40–41, 45.

8. Bloomer, "A Critical Distinction": 56.

9. Joshua Cohen, *Attention: Dispatches from a Land of Distraction* (New York: Random House, 2018).

10. Marina Van Zuylen, *The Plenitude of Distraction* (New York: Sequence Press, 2017), 16–17.

11. Martino Stierli, *Montage and the Metropolis* (New Haven: Yale University Press, 2018), 12.

12. Owen Jones, *Grammar of Ornament* reprint 2006 (Lyon, France: L'Aventurine).

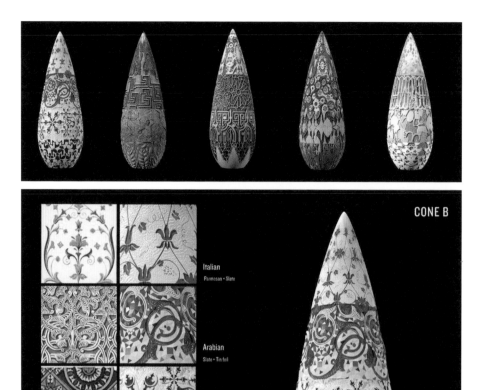

1, 2. *Exquisite Corpse Cones for Harmen Brethouwer, 2015–18.*

3, 4. *Base Flowers*, 2015.

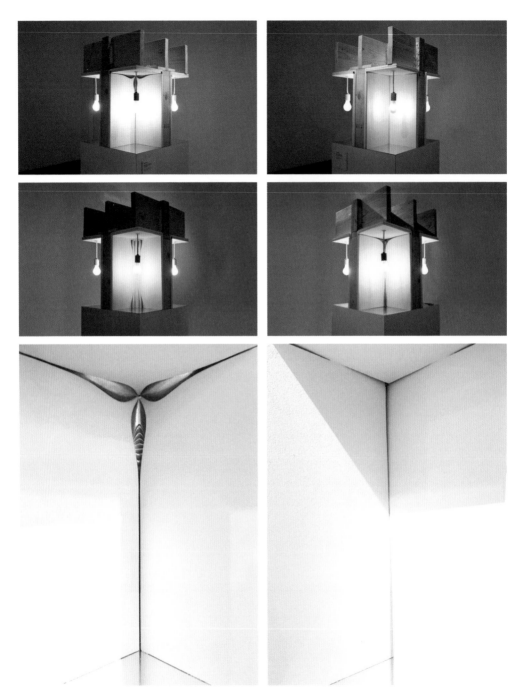

5, 6. *Wall Reveal*, 2016.

7. *DL-1310 Apartment Building,* street view, 2015–19.

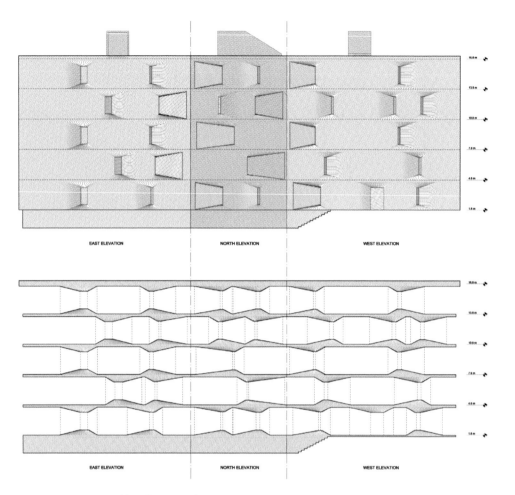

EAST ELEVATION   NORTH ELEVATION   WEST ELEVATION

EAST ELEVATION   NORTH ELEVATION   WEST ELEVATION

8. *DL-1310 Apartment Building,* elevation study, 2015–19.

9. *DL-1310 Apartment Building,* facade construction, 2015–19.

V. PLACES

BODY, SPACE, AND ORNAMENT IN THE WORK OF KENT BLOOMER

Turner Brooks

Turner Brooks is a professor (adjunct) at Yale University. He is a principal of Turner Brooks Architects, based in New Haven.

Kent hovers over my life in so many ways that it is hard to know where to begin. I have learned so much from him, and he is such a great friend.

I have always felt that Kent, more than anyone I know, is attuned to and understands the spatial medium in which we exist: a medium pulsing with life, and from it he extracts the rhythm, beat, and order of his ornament. He metamorphoses ornament out of nature, out of history, and also out of the mysterious invisible ocean of currents and reverberations in the air—all of this coming to Kent, I believe, from his love and deep understanding of both music and physics. A long time ago, Pythagoras said:

> "There is geometry in the humming of strings.
> There is music in the spacing of the spheres."

These vibrations all come together in the creation of ornament to make the space in which we exist more palpable and meaningful in a multitude of ways.

Invoking the concept of *"hovering,"* invokes Kent's brilliant contribution to explaining the meaning of the *body in* space, and as ornament is so much about metamorphosis, I often have imagined Kent metamorphosed into a bat fluttering in space (figure 1). My own syllabus introductory statement for an undergraduate design studio is very much drawn from Kent's sensibility. Invoking the bat, it is titled *In Space,* and reads partly as follows: "Within the intentions of this studio, the bat makes a major contribution to the discussion by his non-visual assessment of space. Always measuring its changing configuration by the beeps he sends out, and the echoes he receives back, he is the ultimately engaged space lunatic aficionado, always locating himself with exactitude within the space, always swerving and never blundering, the space prompting him like a dancer in an elegant ballet." I see the flight of the bat as a physical extension of Kent's design thinking, flowing through, and choreographing our exploration of space. How wonderful it would be to release Kent as the commodore of a swarming flotilla of bats fluttering about in San Carlo alla Quattro Fontane. That might explain this amazing dynamic quality of the space as never before.

Kent was my first teacher at Yale in 1966 along with Charles Moore, who had just taken the reins of the school from Paul Rudolph. Kent was my best, and most memorable teacher. There is little doubt that, had I arrived a year earlier—not even knowing what the now anachronistic parallel rule, or even exactly what a drafting pencil were— I would have been quickly dismissed. But under the regime of Kent and Charles, I mixed plaster, made messes with clay, and was allowed to survive happily in a way that I hadn't experienced since kindergarten.

My relationship with Kent as a student started with the issue of *what is "space"*? He opened the door to this discussion, a discussion that seems weirdly rare to this day, in architectural discourse. Is there even a vocabulary to talk about space? The word "palpable" that I use in a desperate attempt, along with words like *full, diverging and converging, expanding, contracting, currents, whirlpools, back eddies,* hope to describe this illusive subject, but seem hardly adequate. Kent *insisted* space be something that is more than mere empty nothingness, and to prove it, he ordered us students to make a visible, physical manifestation of space. The first project he assigned was the unforgettable *"dominant void,"* with instructions to make a space that was more potent than whatever the material that defined it might be. Sounding like an impossible paradox, something like the quest for the holy grail (many students were left sweating like Lancelots or Gawains, but a few were anointed as Galahads, and the void actually flickered into *real, spatial* existence. Some forty years later I began giving the same project to my own students (figure 2).

What Kent asked from us students was *not a representation of the "real"* but a confrontation with the *"real" itself, an* actual bodily sensation engaging the "haptic" sense, a concept he made famous in his book written with Charles Moore and Buzz Yudell, *Body, Memory, and Architecture.* This focus—especially at the beginning of one's architectural education—was critical in guiding the student to transcend the delusional element with which representation can be fraught, and upon which so much of one's architectural education can be fixated.

The other wonderful thing about Kent and Charles's design studio was that it also ended in a truly "real" project. That was the first building project, a community center in New Zion, Kentucky, an impoverished coal mining area in Appalachia. One of my best

New Zion recollections is that, for a while, Kent and I withdrew from the frenzy of our colleagues heroically and painfully hammering nails through the oak siding to dig the leach field for the septic system. This we did for about a week, becoming more and more obsessed with the beautiful abstraction of a tree spreading out across a meadow, exposing the beautiful red soil of the earth, with trunk turning to branches turning to twigs. This, I felt later on, was a kind of collaboration on a rarified piece of ornament. Another vivid New Zion memory is during an evening break, being in the hazy atmosphere of a bar where Kent played jazz piano. His dancing hands on the keys, the movement of his body, the beat and rhythm, all in retrospect seem so much part of what became his immersion into ornament, where the waves and pulse of sound fill the space with an additional, palpable element. That image of his body immersed in music reminds me to this day of his body language as he explains ornament.

Kent's book, *Body, Memory, and Architecture* (always assigned to my own students), is based on the "haptic sense," or the body's natural desire and ability to locate itself and navigate through space (figure 3a). In his book, Kent describes and demonstrates the haptic extension of spatial perception emanating out from the body. This discussion of the haptic awakened in me, like the wonderful Gaston Bachelard chest from *The Poetics of Sp*ace, drawers within drawers of spatial memories that washed over me, both connecting to past memories, and inspiring me towards future investigations. The theme of the book is about space as experience. The empathy between body and space becomes a reciprocating dance where the body moves through the space, makes discoveries, may become briefly lost, only to find itself again. The message is that space must be choreographed to engage the body. I was brought back to being a kid hiding in my father's overcoat looks out from that cozy bodily wrapper of space that makes the next spatial layer outside feel much more accessible and safe (figure 3b). It invoked childhood books, such as *Goodnight Moon* and *The Runaway Bunny*, where the body ensconced in a cozy container of space is given a heightened meaning by being juxtaposed with the vastness of the space outside (figure 4). In Fra Angelico's *The Annunciation*, architecture is formed directly around the drama of the event. Mary and the angel occupy the intimate space, while Adam and Eve are juxtaposed as outcasts in a gloomy, distant landscape, relegated to wandering off into an immense empty space of the beyond. Just the tip of the angel's wings, that don't quite fit into the architecture, brilliantly unite the two conditions. Or in Labrouste's Bibliothèque Nationale, it seems that the columns are not bearing the weight of the domes above so much as tethering them, and holding them from floating off as if they had been inflated by the subtly profound thoughts emanating upwards from the scholars sitting below. A Sicilian Baroque palazzo reciprocates between the concavity in the building facade and the welcoming convexity of the stair whose curving arms reach out to embrace and pull in the privileged guest, creating a kind of ultimate bodily empathic, "haptic" experience.

Body, Memory, and Architecture allowed how an attic might be a mysterious repository of memory housing Bachelardian chests, the cellar a penumbra's libidinal zone, the living areas in-between, the heart of the house. Space is never neutral, and time represents not only the present, but relates to history and ghosts from the past. Designing—especially a house—for me became much more fun and meaningful after reading this book.

Kent's thinking in general reminds me of the passage from the *Poetics of Space* where Bachelard's protagonist finally imagines hearing the sounds of a minuet coming somewhere from deep within a distant, inaccessible space of the chest. Reality conflates with the imagination. That is perhaps also Kent's prerequisite for the magic of haptic spatial experience.

Early in his career, Kent was involved in constructing amazing individual sculptures made of aluminum beaten over large anvils turned into sinuous, sensual, organic, and often plant-like forms of double-curvature. He worked magic with the continuity of a single surface (something that continues throughout his work) slipping through space, the exterior folded inwards to create a mysterious enclosure, then emerging again to the exterior, before diving back inside yet again, all in a voluptuous rhythm (figure 5a). Several of these works were acquired by the Museum of Modern Art. I see these early singular works very much as the mother plant, or in the image so often invoked by Louis Sullivan, via Ralph Waldo Emerson, of a ". . . seed pod bursting with wings of life," from which thousands of fluttering seeds will be sent floating off into space to plant themselves,

reconfigured into a field condition as a matrix of circuits and connections that is the phenomena of ornament (figure 5b). Kent went
from the singular, individual sculpture to the more universal, ordering
grammar of ornament.

Sullivan continually invoked Emerson's seed analogies in his writing,
merging transcendentalism with his love of democracy. And in between
Emerson and Sullivan there is a critical link to the great, explosive architect Frank Furness. Furness was Emerson's god-child, and very incul-
cated in his thinking. Finding himself in Philadelphia, Sullivan discovers
Furness's buildings, which he describes as speaking to him like "odd
characters on the street." He gets a job working for him between stints
at MIT and, afterwards, the École des Beaux-Arts. Frank Furness's
kinetic drawing of a singular flower depicts it opening up and ready
to discharge its seeds. Furness takes the individual flower and starts to
analyze it geometrically, abstracting it, evolving a system of ornament
(figures 6a–6c). Sullivan later evolves this same methodology further in
his own work.

This evolution was not just a formal, visual issue for any one of
these protagonists, including Kent. The analogy of the seed pod bursting
with wings of life included an idea of engaging with humanity at large.
Sullivan describes his ornament spreading over a building as the triumph
of a new democratic society:

> Rising thus cream-white maiden-like and slender, luxuriant in life and
> joyous as the dawn of wistful spring, this poem of the modern will ever
> daily hail the sun on high and the plodder below with its ceaseless
> song of hope, of joy, of the novel labor of man's hands, of the vast dignity
> and power of man's soul—a song of true democracy and its goal.

I think a fitting description of Kent's later work.

From this more peripheral territory, Kent would say that ornament
seeps in from the "margins," becoming a "frame" for the individual act,
and in so doing may acquire in the end a more subtly surreptitious,
almost secretive, persuasive power than the supposed central act of the
architecture itself.

Kent's studio/shop is a fantastical place to visit (figure 7a–7d). There
is only one computer and copier in the entire office. In the studio itself
the atmosphere is medieval, with mighty anvils and sledge hammers,

various metal cutting implements for making "real" scale work. There are full-scale mock-ups, and parts and pieces of finished projects, their organic order ingeniously broken down into modular components, waiting to be shipped off and put together at their destinations. Ornament is about the whole and the part, which are seamless in Kent's thinking. The wonderful thing to realize is that Kent's own work has evolved into a global phenomenon, and his work is now known and cherished in far-off places across the world.

As Kent has pointed out, in his other great book, *The Nature of Ornament*, the word ornament comes from the Greek word *kosmos*, which has a meaning opposed to "chaos," and is meant to transform or transition contradictory elements into a relationship, acting to mediate difference. Ornament is, as he shows, a universal language with a rhythm and beat that has evolved since the beginning of civilization, and ties us all together. It continues on through whatever style is momentarily percolating, as a fabric that absorbs and lightly floats over the whole history of architecture. Ornament to Kent *is* civilization. He has been the most vital, persistent force in creating its rebirth from the ashes caused by conventional modernism. In this regard, I think of Kent metamorphosed again, appropriately from bat into a phoenix (figure 8).

1. *Metamorphosis of Kent Bloomer.* Collage by the author.

2. Student contemplating the *Dominant Void.*

3a. Drawing by Kent Bloomer from *Body, Memory, and Architecture.*

3b. Overcoat as mediator between the body and its surroundings.

4. The concept of the intimate confronting the immense in the children's book, *The Runaway Bunny.*

5a, 5b. Bloomer's ornament evolving from early-career seedpod to later-career field condition.

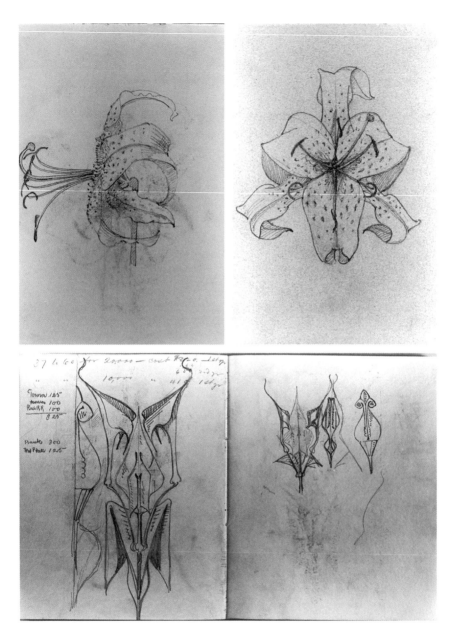

6a-6c. Studies by the author based on drawings by Frank Furness showing evolution from individual plant to ornament.

7a. Anvil from Bloomer studio.

7b. Leaf from Bloomer studio.

7c. Frog from Bloomer studio.

7d. Piece of ornamental pediment for the Chicago Washington Library by Thomas Beeby.

8. *Second Metamorphosis of Kent Bloomer*. Collage by author.

ORGANIC ARCHITECTURE: CHICAGO FROM SULLIVAN TO WRIGHT

Thomas Beeby

Thomas Beeby is chairman emeritus of the Chicago-based firm Hammond, Beeby, Rupert, Ainge, of which he was a founding member. He served as the dean at the Yale School of Architecture from 1985-92, and was part of the "Chicago Seven" architecture group.

Organic architecture, as originated in Chicago, became one of the first forms of Modern architecture precisely because of its roots in ornament. Louis Sullivan advocated that the explicit contemporary use of stylistically based historical precedent was both inauthentic and immoral, for it was blocking the development of an architecture based on contemporary American life. He proposed a new American architecture that grew organically from the uses of the building, its material means of construction, and most importantly, from the spirit of the American people. The forms of this new architecture would grow like a plant from synchronic needs and desires, unfolding in predictable patterns of natural growth based on a geometry that was universal and exact, for it was constructed with a cosmic order true to science and mathematics. Sullivan suggests that this same precise arrangement of the universe was also embedded in the world's ornamentation, an ancient and heretofore irrefutable claim. However, ornament could now be studied in depth through encyclopedic collections available for the first time in the late nineteenth century. The *Grammar of Ornament* (1856) by Owen Jones ecumenically presented all known ornament with remarkable detail, in full color. Jones also prepared naturalistic drawings of foliage with the understanding that they were the basis for the configuration of all botanic ornament. He insisted that these forms had to be abstracted in order to be assimilated into a geometric framework. Having universally evolved over millennia by all societies with varying forms and usages, ornament reflected the mind of man and was interpreted by architects as an artistic medium with profound spiritual significance. Temples were assembled as the built ornamental form of belief systems, reflecting cosmic order through monumental structures. Because of the evolutionary nature of religion and civilization, ancient temples were often abandoned or destroyed. As ruins, their debris was then collected or recycled due to their rich material substance or artistic virtuosity.

Seen in this light, the work of Louis Sullivan is suddenly more legible as a direct reflection of his time. From his writings, it is clear that he wished a spiritually based architecture. He also demanded an architecture that was ordered, achieving a perfection as complete as the greatest works in human history. He pursued an architecture that was absolutely independent and original, free from specific cultural history. He understood that academic architecture since the Renaissance had been based on deduction, with broad general principles of composition, detailed through a canon of conventional components. Sullivan, inversely, created an ornament based on induction, where through the observation of nature, the smallest arrangement of form and geometry could induce a constructed assembly of any magnitude representing the order and power of nature and the cosmos.

The Bible remained a source of inspiration for Western architects like Frank Lloyd Wright. A description of Solomon's Temple is found in the first book of Kings, chapter 6, verses 1–38. Here a meticulous enumeration begins, including methodical measurement of the structure, its elements and finishes, and its fixtures as well. The dimensions suggest a modular origin in their divisibility. *Architectural Record* appeared in 1928 with a review of Wright's then current work: a representation of Unity Temple showed for the first time a regular modular grid drawn over the original plan. Wright offers "The only way to hold all to scale is to adopt a unit-system crossing the paper both ways spaced as pre-determined . . . " At this point, Wright was compelled to justify his design based on its mathematical origin. Unity Temple could be compared to the biblical description of Solomon's Temple, as both buildings are composed of simple geometric volumes aligned along a central axis. Both Temples display a taller central block flanked by a lower volume on three sides, which is secondary in nature. A cube of hierarchical significance is the focus of each Temple. The "Most Holy Place" of Solomon's Temple is the darkened domain of a fearful God, while, conversely, the central spatial cube of Unity Temple is a luminous home for Man living now under the benevolent influence of Nature. Both Temples have massive surrounding walls and are entered through a series of courtyards; both have highly ornamented interiors.

The simple "Root 2" geometric construction of ancient origin is first recorded on clay tablets from Mesopotamia in the eighteenth century B.C. Used in antiquity for surveying, this methodology in ornament became a prevalent practice because it conjoined mathematical repetition with geometrical configuration. The use of repetitive Root 2 progressions could regulate and enrich ornamental patterns involving rotated squares and was found widely in the entire Roman

Empire. The Romans devised the "Ad Quadratum" method of cutting square tiles on their diagonals and combining them with contrasting colored stones to enrich their stone paving patterns, while also enabling prefabrication through standardization. They later introduced circles centered on the crossed diagonals as a further enrichment.

Figures emanating from the geometry of Root 2 and Ad Quadratum progressions inspired a series of symbolic cross types that share the image of an orthogonal cross overlaid by a diagonal one. Once contained within a perfect geometric figure, they became a totemic symbol of Christ for the early Christian church. During the second half of the Middle Ages, the Cosmati, a group of artisans working in the area surrounding Rome, produced a remarkable body of work based on ancient Roman practices. The remaining evidence of their artistry lies in the patterned floors of simple Basilica churches. These pavements display such a high level of geometric sophistication and visual acuity that they often eclipse the architecture that houses them. One of the most provocative aspects of this work is that it is assembled from the spoils of Roman architecture. Thus, the material richness of the Roman Empire was demolished, cut into tiles of modular dimension and reassembled into floor patterns of great beauty. The primary ornamental figure created by the Cosmati was the "Quincunx-in-Square," a powerful geometric design that could be formed into bands through linear repetition, or more significantly expanded into fields along its orthogonal and diagonal axes. Later, the architecture of the Renaissance in Italy during the sixteenth century was similarly based on the study of the remains of the Roman Empire. Architects like Bramante examined, measured, and attempted to decipher their geometric traces and construction methods. Bramante's plan for the miniscule "Tempietto" of 1503 provides evidence of his ability to transform Rome's legacy into a miniaturized state of perfection. Using Roman vocabulary and the Ad Quadratum progression overlaid with concentric circles to organize the plan, he manages to create a perfect, centralized domed chapel. Two schemes for St. Peter's Basilica in Rome, executed first by Bramante and then by Michelangelo, concluded a long study by major Italian architects to perfect the symmetries of centralized churches. Sullivan certainly would have been familiar with European historical development from his study at the Beaux-Arts in

Paris, while Wright at Unity Temple pursued a similar artistic goal
as Bramante had at the Tempietto.

Owen Jones, in his chapter of "Moresque" ornament, offers a drawing explaining harmony in creating patterns. First, he draws a square
grid (declaring it monotonous). Then, in the second drawing, he adds
diagonals at the corners that carry the eye towards the angles, increasing the visual pleasure. Finally, he adds circles centered on the grid,
producing repose or complete harmony, because they properly
balance and contrast the straight, the inclined, and the curved. Franz
Sales Meyer's *Handbook of Ornament* (1888) offers an illustration
in his examples of "Networks" that constructs a "Moorish" diaper
pattern found in Sullivan's ornament. Wright's absence of curved
elements in Unity Temple suggests a formal break in nineteenth-
century theory, although he still composes with a compass to position
elements in plan through ornamental means.

Louis Sullivan's *A System of Architectural Ornament, According
with a Philosophy of Man's Powers* (1922), offers the possibility of
understanding the geometric origins and poetic interpretation of his
ornament, as well as the architecture of Frank Lloyd Wright. However,
if we follow his text and attempt to reconstruct his methodology
exactly, it becomes immediately clear that the illustrated process does
not lend itself to a step-by-step handbook process. Sullivan presents
a numbered sequence of sketches that apparently explain the ornamental configuration. Unfortunately, the geometric scaffolding required to construct the figure is missing, except for the orthogonal and
diagonal axes of the generating square. The substance that the ornament is developed from—its density and its specific properties—are
also missing. However, through a consistent technique of representation, he casts shadows that define the surface relief. From this we can
deduce that the overall ornament is made from a square block whose
depth is approximately one eighth of its length and width. Since most
of Sullivan's ornament was executed in terra-cotta, I have assumed
this is a single, prefabricated terra-cotta block, limited to a twenty-
inch-square dimension by industry standards with a depth of two
and one-half inches. Economic manufacturing requires that there can
be no undercuts in the finished terra-cotta in order to allow consistent
release of the ornament from the formwork. A single Norwegian-
trained sculptor named Christian Schneider executed all of the clay

maquettes for Sullivan's terra-cotta. However, we do not know how important his role was in realizing the final product. Since the exact methodology of preparing the maquette is not recorded, I would suggest that since the final ornament has a systematic layering of surface depth throughout, the method for building relief would be standardized layers of clay, with the figuration achieved through subtraction at each level. This methodology is familiar to architects in constructing contour models to study landforms. I am assuming this procedure is the most expeditious and accurate technique to construct a positive relief model in three dimensions.

My sketches below are constructed with the use of a straightedge, a forty-five-degree triangle, and a compass. They follow Sullivan's sequencing in order to understand his methodology. My first drafting operation (S-1) is to draw a perfect square with orthogonal and diagonal axes to locate the center of the figure. This will become the "focus of energy" for the ornament. From this point, orthogonal and diagonal axes will radiate outward, containing centrifugal energy. Sketch (S-2) constructs a circle first, followed by a smaller circumscribed orthogonal square. My next operation (S-3) requires systematic subdivision of the space within the square frame into a four-by-four grid centered on the figure. A subsequent rotated square establishes the centers of four equal circles that touch circumferences at the orthogonal axes. Next, within each circle, a second circle of lesser diameter establishes edges set in from the perimeter frame. Squaring the four external corners creates a figural void in the configuration of a quatrefoil familiar to Gothic tracery patterns. Sketch (S-4) introduces a central orthogonal square above the quatrefoil, conflicting with the four overlapping central stems, because interpenetration is impossible without local adjustment. This condition is exacerbated in sketch (S-5) by the introduction of bridging elements at the corners of the central square, which would now have to be inserted into the figure to avoid undercuts. In sketch (S-6) a central rotated square outlined in sketch (S-3) is now introduced, connecting to stems formed by the quatrefoil.

The next operation (S-7) adds a layer to the diagonal corner triangles, with its center excavated to form a lattice system extending to the four orthogonal central stems of the arrangement. At this point in the development, sketch (S-8), Sullivan changes from a geometric to an organic mode using forms derived directly from nature expressed in the shape of abstracted leaf patterns. Within the sunken triangles formed by the last operation, he places the diagonal compositions of three leaves in each corner of the central figure. All of the figurations of botanical origin are added to the surface above previous geometric layering. Sketch (S-9) introduces curved tensile organic membranes centered on the diagonal axes above the leaf forms added in the previous sketch. Sullivan's level of development in sketch (S-10) adds a central sunken circular figure. From here, a layer of new organic form grows centrifugally along the central orthogonal axes, balancing the energy of the diagonals of the figure. Finally, Sullivan introduces a rhythmic breakdown of the perimeter frame, creating new interest to the lattice grid with detailed orthogonal edges that add visual activity through elaboration of the linear development accompanied by deep shadows. Sullivan's final drawing (figure 11) renders only one quarter of the figure, forming the summation of the ornamental development of the square block. Now, he adds a series of highly detailed and singular ornaments at the corners and midpoints of the perimeter frame, offering variation to the geometry and marking the sub-centers of energy within the overall composition. The final configuration achieves a balance between orthogonal and diagonal axial energy, creating harmony through the addition of curved elements.

Sullivan's ornament, found in *A System of Ornament*, will serve as a model for the geometric formation of Wright's Unity Temple. I will follow the same process that developed the Sullivan ornament to arrange the building sequentially into spatial layers. Frank Lloyd Wright's autobiography describes the act of designing Unity Temple, but avoids divulging any details of the process involved in actually drawing the building. I will try to reconstruct that progression, again using only a straightedge, a forty-five-degree triangle, and a compass. First, I will in my sketch (W-1), outline the perimeter of the square building, adding the orthogonal and diagonal guidelines to inform future development. From this armature, I next draw outlines of the foundation level of Unity Temple, locating the perimeter wall position, followed by the arrangement for the four central columns. Wright begins to plan according to a strict progression of regulating lines that govern the form of the building through its structure and partitioning. A lattice of guidelines are drawn orthogonally across the figure from the central columns to the perimeter walls, forming reflected piers that provide lateral bracing and define the corners of the building as a differentiated structural unit.

The following sketch (W-2) illustrates the perimeter public access space, located one half-level below the floor of the central sanctuary. A system of stairs is inserted now in the exterior corners leading up to the balcony. A second, one-half-level stair arrangement is systematically grouped at the sides of the four central columns. An internal lattice grid locates smaller piers, added now to support the floor above at the opening for the stairs. Growing asymmetry is developing along the north/south central axis of the plan, suggesting a significant pattern of use variation that affects the overall quadrilateral symmetry of the organization. The third sketch (W-3) illustrates the assembly area of the church, the sanctuary with its cruciform spatial arrangement. The southern arm is occupied by the raised pulpit, flanked by two taller piers rising to the next level, framing the pulpit and supporting the organ loft. Between these piers, a screen of vertical wood members shields the organ pipes and serves as a backdrop for the pulpit. The piers flanking the four central columns are part of a support system for the peripheral alcove balconies raised one half-level above. On the north, east, and west sides, the piers only rise to railing height, however their alignment forms a lattice system of arrangement that breaks down the scale of the central room.

Sketch (W-4) is the reflected ceiling plan of the previous plan locating the position of the four suspended lighting fixtures in the central sanctuary space. A grid of coffered skylights overhead is seen in relation to the fixtures and the four central columns, as well as a system of lineal ornamental trim located on the ceiling of the three seating alcoves. This is the first indication of an overall three-dimensional ornamental strategy breaking down the traditional handling of surfaces and edges by Wright. The enclosing wood screen for the organ loft is positioned in plan on the south side by a central circular guideline that is constructed touching the diagonal corners of the four central columns. Wright sets back the balcony rails parallel to the face of the columns shown in sketch (W-5). Here, the perimeter wall is reduced to a systematically undulating ribbon that continuously encloses this level. Complete quadrilateral symmetry is still broken by the enclosure of the organ loft, continuing to maintain the hierarchical

significance of the pulpit below. The location of the external colon-
nade illustrates the elevational strategy of the central cube but cannot be seen yet from the interior. In sketch (W-6), the ceiling plan
reveals a perfect quadrilateral figure that is truly symmetrical. By
eliminating the stair volumes at the corners, the perimeter wall now
forms an external cruciform. A centered rotated square bisecting the
four columns places the limits of the dimensions of the roof. The axes
of the central coffered beams extend centrifugally to align with the
external square columns now visible from the interior through the
glass window wall that encloses the sanctuary beneath the ceiling.
A wood trim system divides each alcove ceiling into rectangular panels
with corners displaced by the four central columns. The roof plan,
sketch (W-7), is a remarkably clear diagram, absolutely symmetrical.
At the corner of the central roof parapet, all the volumes of the
composition intersect. The vertical structural loads above the ceiling
descend onto the four central columns, passing through the sanctuary
to the foundations below.

The section (W-8) illustrates the central cube, imbedded in the
cruciform base of the upper balcony level, then dropping into the overall square volume of the primary seating area. The displacement of the
central service level below the sanctuary, down one level, creates
the characteristic one-half-level disjunction of space throughout,
activating the room with a diagonal oscillation that is palpable. The
elevation (W-9) offers a clear image of a protected central cube, illuminated by clerestory windows behind colonnades on each face of the
central cruciform assembly space serviced by the four lower stair
towers at the corners. The outlined rotated square positions the plane
of the ceiling, which divides the heavens above from the world of
Man, sheltered within the protective walls rising from the earth. The
cosmic implications of both Sullivan's and Wright's designs become
more apparent when expanded through ornamental extension. If
Sullivan's ornament is repeated nine times on its center (figure 21),
there appears a field with subordinate lattice grids centered on the
circular focus of each ornament. When single bands of Sullivan's
ornaments are compared to the section of Unity Temple, which
through mirroring or reflecting is translated along a single axis to form
a band (figure 22), the similarities are striking. The unfolded central
sanctuary reveals the thought behind Wright's placement of applied

wood strips wrapping the four columns of the sanctuary when viewed orthogonally. While the trim forms a partial field disappearing around the corner of the column, it is now seen to be conjoined with its opposite counterpart, providing two-dimensional symmetry across the space. As one turns rotationally to view the room from its center, these colored panels become a single folded panel that rhythmically repeats, first orthogonally, then diagonally, as the eye circles the sanctuary. This unfolding process of disclosing the central cube of Unity Temple explains the power of its arrangement, where plan, section, and elevation merge into one rhythmic whole. Finally, I would posit the theory that both Wright and Sullivan saw themselves as Prophets of the Modern at its very inception, godlike figures who arranged the built world into cosmic perfection. I believe that through the ancient process of ornamentation, they managed to create a world based on the forms and forces of nature with no direct precedence of one known architectural style. Instead, they both drew inspiration and methods from multiple sources of ancient origin that were universal in architecture but never codified into one particular style. In that sense, Sullivan and Wright are both perfect representatives of nineteenth-century Romanticism, with its encyclopedic interests and polyvalent production. A biblical illustration by William Blake (1794) captures the essence of their faith in absolute measure to blend perfection of form with spiritual significance.

Afterword

It is an honor for me to participate in this volume celebrating Kent Bloomer on his retirement from Yale. We have collaborated on numerous projects and I have always been impressed by his enormous talent, intellectual focus, and technical virtuosity. There has been no one in this country who has pursued the artistry and theory of ornament with more passion and success than Kent Bloomer. He has been a voice in the wilderness against the trivialization and commercialization of architecture within our lifetime. We are all deeply indebted to him, but especially those of us who have had the honor to be his colleague at the Yale School of Architecture.

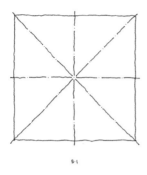

S-1.*

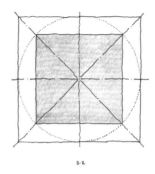

S-2.

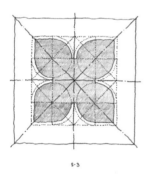

S-3.

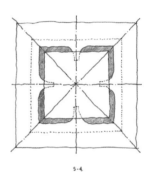

S-4.

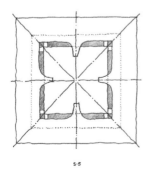

S-5.

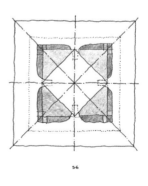

S-6.

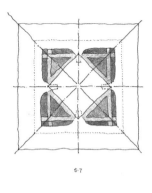

S-7.

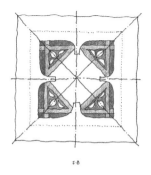

S-8.

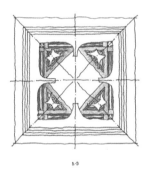

S-9.

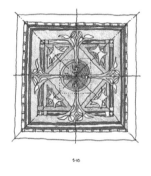

S-10.

* Drawings by author unless otherwise indicated.

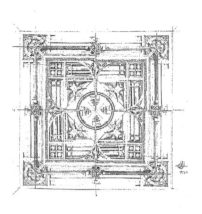

Louis H. Sullivan and Howard Van Doren
Shaw, *A System of Architectural Ornament*.
Chicago: 1924.

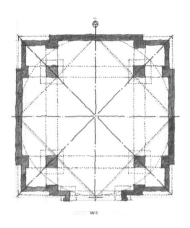

W-1.

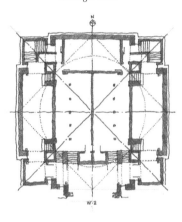

W-2.

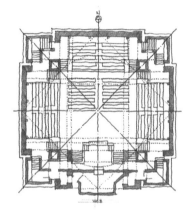

W-3.

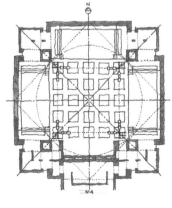

W-4.

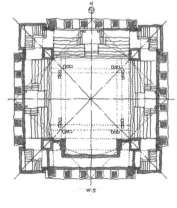

W-5.

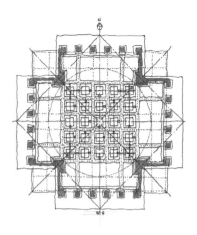

W-6.

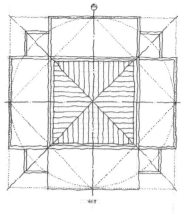

W-7.

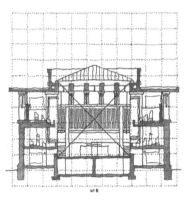

W-8.

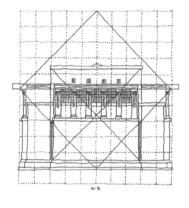

W-9.

Louis H. Sullivan and Howard Van Doren Shaw, *A System of Architectural Ornament*. Chicago: 1924. Collage by author.

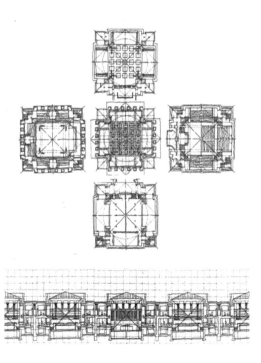

W-Compiled.

William Blake, *Europe, a Prophecy*, handcolored engraved plate. Lambeth: Printed by Will. Blake, 1794. From the Lessing J. Rosenwald Collection, Library of Congress, Washington, D.C..

ON TEACHING ORNAMENT TODAY

Kent Bloomer

Kent Bloomer is the principal and founder of the Bloomer Studio, and has served as its chief designer since 1965. He is also a retired professor of architecture at Yale University, where he has taught since 1966.

Among the many questions that have surfaced in my seminar on the theory and design of ornament, the most crucial one turned out to be, "what precisely *is* ornament *per se*"? How does its essential identity fundamentally differ from decoration, pattern, applied "art"-work, and so forth?

I had assumed that by viewing, sketching, and designing, the particular "makeup" of ornament would become obvious. That was my personal experience. "See what it is and what it does!" But this approach became thornier than I had anticipated. Teaching ornament in the late twentieth century, and today, requires sorting through a ragbag of prejudices, diversions, and misnomers that had to be challenged, one at a time. Thousands of years of conventional knowledge about ornament was waylaid after WWII as a consequence of its removal as a subject of discourse within our schools of design.

My own study of ornament began by being born in New York in 1935. The then five-year-old Chrysler Building, the forty-year-old Grand Central Terminal, and the myriad ornamented lobbies and facades were my first observations of a unique type of figuration. Before attending college, I read ornament in Havana, Casablanca, London, and Barcelona. I was amazed by the interior walls of Garnier's Paris Opera House and wanted to find out how such intricacy had been derived.

I chose MIT and signed up for physics, which I thought was fundamental, but slowly drifted towards the architecture department and their "media" labs led by Gyorgy Kepes from the New Bauhaus of Chicago. They were places to fabricate and critique visual experiments. However, in a lecture hall, I was alarmed when a fleeting image of the entrance base of Sullivan's Carson, Pirie, Scott and Company Building flashed on, only to be quickly edited by tilting the projector upward with the instructor's explanation that the street-level architecture of the building was of no importance (figure 1). "Look only at the upper floors!" Rushing to the library, I discovered more astonishing examples of Sullivan's work, augmented by texts.

At the end of my fourth year, I transferred to Yale where I spent three more years in the "labs" of Albers's program exploring symmetry operations, color theory, visual semiotics, architecture, and sculpture. In the airwaves, Rudolph Arnheim was preparing his seminal book, *Visual Thinking,* published in 1969. Visual thinking, alongside verbal and numerical thought, was achieving full citizenship in academe. After graduating, I taught for five years at Carnegie Tech alongside William Huff who had attended the Hochschule für Gestaltung in Ulm, thus updating my "New Bauhaus" research.

In my own shop I was exploring the syntax between sculpture and walls, such as the bas-relief for Pittsburgh's Temple Rodef Shalom (figure 2); the sculpture *Intersection*; and the lobby ornament for the Northshore Plaza in Pittsburgh.

I returned to Yale in 1966 to teach in the architecture school. Ornament was also in the airwaves. George Hersey's 1976 book, *Pythagorean Palaces*, examined Renaissance systems of cosmic geometry; the entire 1977 issue of the University of Pennsylvania's *Via III* featured ornament. Vincent Scully referred to ornament as the "decoration of construction." The academic climate for excavating and pursuing ornament seemed to be alive and well at Yale, despite its spooky absence from architecture programs and new architecture design worldwide.

So, in 1977, I decided to introduce a seminar titled "The Theory and Design of Ornament." This seminar included analyzing historic ornament found in the extraordinary nineteenth-century encyclope-dias, such as Owen Jones's seminal *Grammar of Ornament*, Racinet's *Polychrome Ornament*, and Dolmetsch's *Treasury of Ornament* (figure 3). These encyclopedias advanced our knowledge by illustrating fig-ures of ornament gathered from the entire world, regardless of their age, culture, politics, or technology. Ornament's pervasive and unique vocabulary, together with its timeless identity, became clearly evident. Our class discussions were further fueled by theoretical works such as Semper's *Four Elements of Architecture*, Ruskin's *Seven Lamps of Architecture*, Riegl's *Problems of Style*, Goodyear's *Grammar of the Lotus*, and Hamlin's systematic *History of Ornament*.

The seminar's first axiom was: *In order to perform, figures of ornament must be systematically engaged with the material, the form, and the structural logic of the thing being ornamented.* I called that thing a "holder." The figures of ornament, by themselves, were not considered to be independent or autonomous works of art that could be exhibited and isolated within the white precinct of a museum.

At first, the design work of the seminar studied ways to distribute conventional figures of ornament into surfaces of buildings or bowls. Systems of geometry and types of animated elements were examined.

Those first steps carried the early seminars through a history of architectural styles, revealing that ornament thrived in the thresholds or liminal regions of the holders. *This was an important finding,* although it failed to explain the essential purpose of ornament per se. The critical question then became: "What particular type of content, presumably absent in a holder, is gained by incorporating ornament?"

Unfortunately, in the mid-nineteenth-century encyclopedias— and especially in *The Grammar of Ornament*—figurations of ornament were mostly illustrated on colored plates which did not include their holders. That separation compromised our project because we could not study the connections, or syntax, which unified the figures with their holders. Nevertheless, the details inside those illustrated parcels, especially their intimate systems of organization, could be carefully analyzed and deconstructed, which illustrated that a very limited number of geometric figures, or "tropes," were common to thousands of examples throughout the world. *This was another important finding* because it visually articulated the abstract details of a common, or very specific, family of figuration evident in the history of world ornament.

For example, a large percentage of figures were either dynamically geometric, or were geometry morphing into abstractions of life-forms. The most common was the geometric leaf-form which appeared in a majority of the plates. The western world abstracted those forms from the lotus, the acanthus, the palm, and, for Louis Sullivan, the oak leaf. Early Chinese forms differed by alluding to serpent shapes. Islam favored pointed stars and leaf-like "arabesques." But those exceptions seemed to prove the rule. I personally suspected the seminal life-forms were more "energy-diagrams" than culturally specific symbols (which many became over time). Essentially, they were sensual constructs of natural forces.

Indeed, the small clusters of animated foliage, entangled with elements of pure geometry, exhibited an interaction of natural and man-made forces (figure 4) in the same way that an entire body of ornament does when it becomes entangled with the stationary form of its particular holder.

In the early twentieth century, ornament also began to be described as a language with its own "alphabet" and grammar. Henri Focillon, in his 1934 masterpiece, *The Life of Forms in Art,* wrote in a chapter entitled, "Forms in the Realm of Space," that ornament was, "perhaps the first alphabet of our human thought to come into close contact with space."[1] The survival and persistence of that alphabet's classical tropes (figure 5) suggest that our all-too-relentless pursuit of innovation may not apply to the content of ornament. Granting that technical innovations do transform the materials and shapes of the holders, and thus the formation of the complete ornamented product, the limited alphabet within ornament confirms its identity as a conventionalized language. *This was one more important finding in the seminar.*

For example, ornament's adherence to a rigorous system of repetition, with repeating phrases of two and a half or more cycles[2] reveals one of its most universal, systematic, and definitive tropes. Ornament's portions of regular repetition, without firm beginnings or endings, evoke moments of infinity (apeiron) or the unlimited, which in early Greek philosophy was a property of chaos. It was the opposite of order. Thus, ornament's practice of relentless parcels of repetition could be read as visual moments of chaos. Yet, the axis of repetition is immediately challenged by being divided into phrases which, by themselves, express beginnings and endings, zigs and zags, spirals, fractals, syncopation and metamorphosis. Those intervening figures order the composition into rhythmized motions of order, unity, and resolution. Harmonic orchestration is visualized within those phrases in which animated shapes perform a dance with and around the relentless stream of infinity. Lively expressions of counterpoint play in all scales of ornament, whether upon the smallest bowl or the largest building.

The conflation of the terms "decoration" and "ornament," in dictionaries and everyday parlance, has further confused the discourse on ornament. While the content of decoration, which is concerned with propriety, festivity, fashion, and social order, may locate or distribute ornament, it may also locate or distribute paintings, flowers, furniture, and light fixtures which are not figures of ornament. For example, one may decorate a room with white walls, but where is the ornament? Ornament employs specific figures derived from forces found in nature-at-large, rather than society-at-small.

Investigating the confusion between decoration and ornament led to a collaboration with the art historian, ornamenter, musician, and librarian, Kresten Jespersen, who, in 1988, had written the first dissertation in the U.S on Owen Jones's *Grammar*. Precisely because ornament's alphabet and grammar remained fundamentally unchanged over thousands of years, it was obvious that we had to visit the *origin* of the Latin word, "ornamentum," to discern its primordial function and to detect why it came into being in the first place. It was in the *Etymologies of Isidore of Seville*, written around 670 A.D., within the last century of Plato's Academy, that a coherent formulation of the word "ornament" finally made perfect sense and aligned with the visual properties we found in the seminar to have been constant from antiquity to the present.[3]

The title of Book XIII in the *Etymologies* is "The cosmos and its parts." Part 1 of paragraph i is titled, "The world (De mundo)," and states:

> *the world consists of the sky and the land, the sea*
> *and the creations . . . within them . . . 'World' (mundus)*
> *is named thus in Latin by the philosophers, because it*
> *is in eternal motion (motus), as are the sky, the sun,*
> *the moon, the air, the seas. Thus, no rest is allowed*
> *to its elements; on this account it is always in motion.*[4]

Part 2 in the same paragraph continues,

> *Whence to Varro the elements seemed to be animate,*
> *"Because," he says, "they move of their own accord."*
> *But the Greeks adopted a term for world (mundus, also*
> *meaning "cosmetics") derived from 'ornament,' on*
> *account of the diversity of elements and the beauty*
> *of the heavenly bodies. They call it κόσμος, which*
> *means "ornament," for with our bodily eyes we see*
> *nothing more beautiful than the world.*[5]

In ancient Greek, *kosmetikos* meant *kosmos* made visible or audible, and sensually harmonic. For Isidore, that required making the motions within the *kosmos* visible, harmonic, and therefore beautiful.

In ancient Latin, the transitive verb, *ornare*, means *to adorn*, which also meant *to equip* or *furnish* something. This meaning implies, on the one hand, that ornament is auxiliary and requires a recipient or a holder, such as a building or a bowl, and, on the other hand, that ornament, once delivered, becomes the property of the equipped holder. The act of ornamenting, thus, involves furnishing the holder with *kosmos*.

The terms *ornament* and *cosmos* were interchangeable in Isidore's *Etymology*. Both visualized activity in the sky, the sun, the moon, the air, and the seas. Isidore's list of the specific parts of the cosmos occupies the rest of Book XIII. For Isidore, the ancient Greek vision of ornament was an astronomic spectacle of the totality, (the gestalt) of forces to be witnessed primarily, but not exclusively, in the outer reaches in the firmament at the edge of the world-at-large.

For the designer of ornament today, Isidore's chapter proposes a compact summation of the motions found *in the natural environment*, beginning with heavenly bodies, followed by clouds, oceans, and rivers in second place, and earthly forms in third place. Isidore allows, furthermore, that those motions also exist within the smallest of earthly parts, such as "the finest dust" and "the atoms." Paragraph ii in Book XIII is titled "Atoms (De atomis")" and states,

> Atoms . . . are said to fly through the void of the
> entire world in unceasing motion and to be carried
> here and there like the finest dust motes that may be
> seen pouring in through the window in the sun's rays.[6]

Note once again his persistent emphasis on *motion*. The designer can visually abstract those motions with repetitions, spirals, zig zags, fractals, plants, animated geometry or, as in Sullivan, within the turbulence of dense foliage. Significantly, Isidore's inventory of the "Cosmos and its parts" does not mention man-made objects. His Kosmos only addresses the moving parts found in nature. One question for the designer would have to be: "What sort of details, places, or material systems belonging to the holder might provide the connectivity to mediate between the motions of ornament innate to the natural environment and the stabilities of enclosed space and construction innate to its holders?" Such connectivity must be located in places of transition such as inside to outside, roof to sky, wall to ceiling, rims of glassware and pottery, and, occasionally, they may be the dead center of buildings and bowls. Places of transition are sites of convergence able to address two or more places simultaneously. They are also realms in which the energy of ornament's motions converges with the gravity with-in and with-out its holders.

*Conclusion: Some Images Regarding the Realms of Transition
and Convergence*

1. Within the *Realm of Classical Construction* the columns and ribs
of classical and Gothic architecture convey the fixed power of stationary structural support running upward into the fleeting expressions
of motion within the ornament above, for example see sketches on
page 206: Parthenon's rhythm; Classical orders; Gothic nave; York
West Window; Facade of the Wainwright Building (figure 6)

2. Within the *Public Realm*, the dome above the pathway of the
Kashan Bazaar provides a moment of repose that ascends from
the ground to the sky through a field of ornamented *marquanas*
(figure 7).

3. Within the *Realm of Space*, a vertical cylinder of space within the
Kresge Chapel (figure 8) and an immense cubic void beyond the
entrance to the Slover Library (figure 9) harbor thresholds and fields
of ornament illuminated by natural light from above.

4. Within the *Realm of Time*, the hemispheres upon a small clay
vessel (figure 10) are ornamented by singular spirals converging at the
dead centers of four sides. The geometric precision of the repeating
spiral serves as a trope of ornament upon a holder which still remains
meaningful today, six thousand years later!

Notes
1. Henri Focillon, *The Life of Forms in Art* (New York: Zone Books, 1992), 66.
2. More than two linear cycles of a geometric figure are optically required to signify an
extended continuity of repetition. The gestalt of two repeats standing alone can congeal
into a singularity wherein two complete figures signify a unified and complete "pair."
3. John Kresten Jespersen, "The Ornament, Decoration and Color of Owen Jones: Studies
in the Art and Science of Architectural Design," PhD diss., Brown University, c. 1988.
Edited in 2010 for the World Wide Web as "Owen Jones and the Conventionalization
of Ornament."
4. *The Etymologies of Isidore of Seville*, ed. and trans. Stephen A. Barney, W.J. Lewis, J.A.
Beach, and Oliver Berghof (Cambridge, England: Cambridge University Press, 2006), 271.
5. Ibid.
6. Ibid.

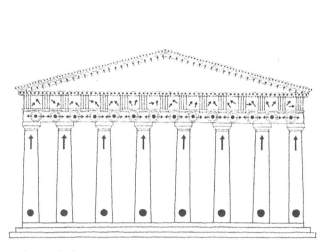

Parthenon's rhythm

Classical orders

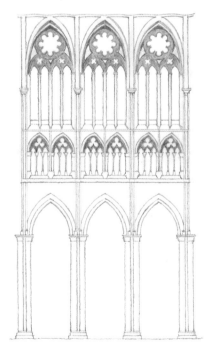

Gothic nave

York West Window

1. *Carson, Pirie, Scott Building.* Louis H. Sullivan: Chicago, IL. Photograph by Beyond My Ken.

2. Rodef Shalom Congregation Bas Relief. Kent Bloomer: Pittsburgh, PA. Photograph by Kent Bloomer.

3. H. Dolmetsch, Arabian-Moresque mosaic work in *Der Ornamentenschatz; ein Musterbuch stilvoller Ornamente aus allen Kunstepochen.* Stuttgart: 1887.

4. Owen Jones, Cloisonné enamel vase in *The Complete "Chinese Ornament."* London: 1867.

5. *Greek, Chinese, and Mayan Keys.* Drawing by Kent Bloomer.

6. *Wainwright Building.* Louis H. Sullivan: Chicago, IL. Photograph by Cervin Robinson.

7. *Kashan Bazaar*. Kashan, Iran. Photograph by Mehdi Sahraei.

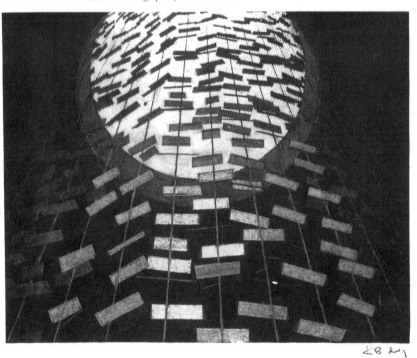

8. *Altar Screen for Kresge Chapel at MIT*. Harry Bertoia: Cambridge, MA. Drawing by Kent Bloomer.

9. *Slover Library*, Newman Architects: Norfolk, VA. Photograph by Peter Aaron/OTTO.

10. *Danube Bowl*, biconical vessel, Cucuteni-Trypillia culture, 4050–3850 B.C. Drawing by Kent Bloomer.

AFTERWORD

Deborah Berke

Deborah Berke is an architect, educator, and the Dean of the Yale School of Architecture.
She is the founder of the New York-based architecture firm Deborah Berke Partners.

Kent Bloomer has been a remarkable force and presence at the Yale School of Architecture.

In fact, in some ways I owe my presence here to him, as on my first visit to Yale as a guest critic on first-semester reviews, he and I got into an argument about ornament. My first mistake was in being opposed to it on general principles; my second was in equating it with—and calling it—decoration. I have since matured. As you can imagine, it was a knock-down, drag-out kind of disagreement that lasted the entire day.

I think the students enjoyed it—they must have, because several weeks later Tom Beeby, then dean, invited me to apply for an open position here as a junior member of the design faculty. I'm still here, so I thank you both; but today I really thank Kent. It has been a pleasure to work at your side over the many past years. I admire your work, your teaching, your passionate convictions, and the depth of your knowledge. You're a Yale man . . .

In fact,

Kent Bloomer is a man with a Yale MFA
Those degrees aren't something they just give away
He briefly went teaching at Carnegie Mellon
A good early workout for his cerebellum
Kent also knows everything about symmetry
But I reckon he learned that while at MIT

Kent's taught at Yale since 1966
Studios and seminars were all in his mix
Way back in the day Kent taught in the core
But over the years there've been courses galore
Geometry, Drawing and Visual In-queer-y
And even Viz II taught with gusto and theory
Furniture and Ornament Theory and Design
3D Form and Materials combined
Basics of Visual Perception, Spatial Morphology
And Advanced Basic Design Methodology
Spatial Language, an introduction
3D and 2D representation instruction
Famous for the course Design Fundamentals
Repeating patterns and their differentials

Design and production in alu-minium
Fundamentals of Form and the Space-time continuum

Kent doesn't really do polite mindless chatter
He much prefers discussions of substantive matter
Let's think of the ways we know Kent is smart
He understands physics and makes complex art
At LACMA and MoMA his work has been shown
The Carnegie Museum and at the Hirsh—hone
Also in DC he's shown at the Smithsonian
And at Yale's Art Gallery, up on a podium

Bloomer Studio collaborates with Stern, Pelli, and Newman
His ornament makes their work that much more human
He did two gates at Yale Chemistry and Rosenkranz
With patterns of steel are these portals enhanced
Elsewhere we see wings, leaves, and foliated trellises
Ornament applied with intellectual zealousness

His books include one called *Mimetic Rivalry*
With advice on form that is more than advisory
The Nature of Ornament contains pattern conjecture
And with Moore he did *Body, Memory, and Architecture*
Summerson's *Heavenly Mansions* has Kent's introduction
Perspecta 17 has his Mexican ruins and construction

His drink's a martini, the Barnacle's his boat,
Thanks to "glide reflection" it stays afloat
We are happy to welcome many Bloomer kin
Kent's the honoree but Nona's the linchpin
Today Hastings is filled with architects and friends
Family, and scholars and setters of trends
Artists and makers, design world big names
From carvers of stones to animators of games
Scientists, makers of jazz, and musicians
Craftsmen, cosmologists, rhythmic physicians
For his teaching and his scholarship on ornamentation
Let's rise and thank Kent with a standing ovation!

Image Credits

Mari Hvattum
1. Hathi Trust/New York Public Library. Public Domain. https://hdl.handle.net/2027/nyp.33433081594636
2. Private Collection.

Stacey Sloboda
2. V&A, London. Prints, Drawings & Paintings Collection. Open Access.
3. Bridgeman Images.
4. Metropolitan Museum of Art. Harris Brisbane Dick Fund, 1934. Open Access.
5. Houghton Library, Harvard University. Open Access.
6. Library Company of Philadelphia.
7. Metropolitan Museum of Art. John Stewart Kennedy Fund, 1918. Open Access.
8. Museum purchase, made possible by an anonymous donor, 1993 E84004.
   © Peabody Essex Museum.

Richard Prum
2-3. Michael Digiorgio
5. Brett Benz

Guru Dev Khalsa
1. Jessie Peña, AZ. Home Drone
3–8. Michael Jennings Photography

Willie Ruff
1. NASA/JPL-Caltech.

Gary He
15. David Lamb Photography.
24. Peter Aaron/OTTO.

Douglas Cooper
1. Google Art Project/Fondazione Musei Senesi (Collection). Public Domain.

Emer O'Daly
2. Generated by software written by Professor David Eck. Department of Mathematics and Computer Science, Hobart and William Smith Colleges https://math.hws.edu/eck
3. Public Domain.
6. Bibliothèque-Musée de L'Opéra National de Paris-Garnier (Library)/De Agostini Editore.

Turner Brooks
4. Private Collection.

Thomas Beeby
23. Lessing J. Rosenwald Collection, Library of Congress, Washington, DC. https://www.loc.gov/item/48031341/. Open Access.

Kent Bloomer
1. Beyond My Ken, Wikimedia Commons.
3. Public Domain.
4. Public Domain.
6. Cervin Robinson.
7. Mehdi Sahraei.
9. Peter Aaron/OTTO.